PLC+

Better Decisions and Greater Impact by Design

What's this book about?

- Provides a brief history of PLCs
- Introduces the PLC+ framework questions and crosscutting themes
- Shows the PLC+ in action in various settings

When do I need this book?

- You want to understand the purpose of PLCs
- You want to learn a new framework for effective PLCs
- You want to reinvigorate and increase the impact of your existing PLC

The PLC+ Playbook

A Hands-On Guide to Collectively Improving Student Learning

What's this book about?

- Provides a practical, hands-on guide to implementing the full PLC+ cycle
- Guides PLC+ group members through 22 modules as they answer the five guiding questions and focus on the four crosscutting themes
- Offers modules comprising an array of tools that support implementation of the PLC+ framework

When do I need this book?

- You want to plan and implement the PLC+ framework in collaborative settings
- You want to implement the PLC+ model step by step in your own PLC

The PLC+ Activator's Guide

What's this book about?

- Provides guidance for the PLC+ team activators

When do I need this book?

- You are a PLC+ activator and want to do the best possible job for your group
- You are an activator and want to pre-plan the implementation of your PLC+
- You need help to guide the group in overcoming obstacles or having difficult conversations

PLCN203A9

THE PLC+ ACTIVATOR'S GUIDE

THE PLC+ ACTIVATOR'S GUIDE

DAVE NAGEL

JOHN ALMARODE

DOUGLAS FISHER

NANCY FREY

KAREN FLORIES

FOR INFORMATION:

Corwin
A SAGE Company
2455 Teller Road
Thousand Oaks, California 91320
www.corwin.com

SAGE Publications Ltd.
1 Oliver's Yard
55 City Road
London EC1Y 1SP
United Kingdom

SAGE Publications India Pvt. Ltd.
B 1/I 1 Mohan Cooperative Industrial Area
Mathura Road, New Delhi 110 044
India

SAGE Publications Asia-Pacific Pte. Ltd.
18 Cross Street #10-10/11/12
China Square Central
Singapore 048423

Director and Publisher, Corwin Classroom: Lisa Luedeke
Editorial Development Manager: Julie Nemer
Associate Content Development Editor: Sharon Wu
Marketing Manager: Deena Meyer
Production Editor: Veronica Stapleton Hooper
Copy Editor: Karen E. Taylor
Typesetter: C&M Digitals (P) Ltd.
Proofreader: Dennis W. Webb
Indexer: Jean Casalegno
Cover Designer: Gail Buschman

Printed in the United States of America

Library of Congress Cataloging-in-Publication Data

Names: Nagel, Dave, author. | Almarode, John, author. | Fisher, Douglas, author. | Frey, Nancy, 1959- author. | Flories, Karen, author.

Title: The PLC+ activator's guide / Dave Nagel, John T. Almarode, Douglas Fisher, Nancy Frey, Karen T. Flories.

Description: First edition. | Thousand Oaks, California : Corwin, [2020] | Includes bibliographical references and index.

Identifiers: LCCN 2020001985 | ISBN 9781544384047 (spiral bound)

Subjects: LCSH: Professional learning communities. | Teachers—Professional relationships.

Classification: LCC LB1731 .N21 2020 | DDC 370.71/1—dc23

LC record available at https://lccn.loc.gov/2020001985

This book is printed on acid-free paper.

21 22 23 24 10 9 8 7 6

CONTENTS

LETTER FROM THE AUTHORS

Dear Educator,

In our collective years of experience, we have never come across anyone who works in education who has said, "I have too much spare time on my hands, so I would love to attend another meeting." In our schools and classrooms, time is at a premium. If the school day begins at or around 8:00 a.m. and dismissal occurs somewhere on or around 3:00 p.m., this gives us a seven-hour school day at best. When you remove the time devoted to transitions, lunch, and the logistics of being in school (e.g., packing up, unpacking, announcements), those seven hours quickly tick away. We are not saying that transitions, lunch, and the logistics are not important, but we are highlighting the need for protecting our time outside of instructionally focused efforts. This brings us back to the above comment about "another meeting." As we pointed out in *PLC+: Better Decisions and Greater Impact by Design* and *The PLC+ Playbook, Grades K–12: A Hands-On Guide to Collectively Improving Student Learning* (Fisher, Frey, Almarode, Flories, & Nagel, 2020a, 2020b, Corwin), your PLC meetings may have lost their efficiency and effectiveness, relegating them to the category of "another meeting." We are confident in this hypothesis simply because you chose to read this guide for *activators*. For that we are grateful; we believe that the ideas in this guide will serve as a catalyst to the collective and successful work of you and your colleagues—work that will take you beyond the feeling that PLC+ just means another meeting to endure.

With that said, we want to share two very important things we are passionate about when it comes to PLCs:

1. We are passionate about helping educators leverage their expertise to lead and develop actions that support their PLC+.

2. We are passionate about supporting the work of educators as they strive to maximize their impact on student learning.

As we engaged in the development and implementation of PLC+, we immediately recognized the difference between those PLC meetings that translated our two passions into action and those PLC meetings that encountered challenges in moving professional conversations, and thus learning, forward in schools and classrooms. In some conference rooms, PLC meetings digressed into topics not related to the upcoming teaching and learning. In other grade-level planning sessions, PLCs did not address the root cause or underlying challenge impacting the students' learning outcomes. They missed the white elephant in the room, or the pink gorilla—whatever you want to call it. And finally, some of the PLCs spun their wheels on a particular topic, draining the desire and passion of the team. After all, simply staring at the challenge or opportunity, almost admiring it, can be exhausting.

Thus enters the *activator* and the very purpose of *The PLC+ Activator's Guide*. One way PLC+ teams can proactively avoid some of these and other common pitfalls is by having a strong *activator*. Activation, one of the crosscutting values of the PLC+, was intentionally built into the framework to highlight the importance of moving the dialogue and discussion forward in an intentional and purposeful way.

1. We must keep the **equity** of access and opportunity for learning at the forefront of each PLC+ collaborative team meeting.

2. We must ensure that **activation** of the dialogue is provoked by the five questions and is carried out in such a way that the work of the PLC+ is accelerated, not hindered or impeded.

3. We must develop learning experiences that make our **expectations** for learning clear to all students.

4. And finally, the collaborative work of the PLC+ should leverage our **individual efficacy** into **collective teacher efficacy**.

The PLC+ Activator's Guide is broken down into eight parts with each part supporting your development as an *activator*. The purpose of the guide is to create a pathway for this activation to take place with regularity and consistency within a PLC+. Let us be clear—this guide seeks to build capacity within each member of the PLC+ team such that, over time, *all* members will recognize activation points in the work of the PLC+ team and provoke dialogue and discussion around the five PLC+ guiding questions in a way that continuously moves the learning of both students and teachers forward.

We welcome you to the role of *activator* as you begin your journey through *The PLC+ Activator's Guide*. Over the eight parts of this book, we will present new content while incorporating key concepts from the core PLC+ book and *The PLC+ Playbook*. Together, we will engage in an interactive exploration and analysis of the why, how, and what of PLC+ through the eyes of an *activator*. Although all protocols in *The PLC+ Playbook* were designed to be used collaboratively in your PLC+, we will highlight many, but not all, in our journey to develop *activators*. Thank you for your commitment and service to teaching and learning.

Dave, John, Douglas, Nancy, and Karen

ABOUT THE AUTHORS

Dave Nagel, MS Ed, is a full-time Professional Learning Consultant with Corwin. Dave has been a professional developer both nationally and internationally since 2003, working deeply with schools in the areas of assessment, improved grading and feedback actions to promote student learning, instructional leadership, and effective collaboration focused on ensuring both student and adult learning. Dave has done significant research related to effective collaboration and has developed practical instruments to assist collaborative teams in monitoring their adult behaviors to ensure having an effective team. In addition to his professional development work with teachers, leaders, community members, and other stakeholders, Dave is also a frequent speaker at state and national conferences and has contributed to several books, including *Effective Grading Practices for Secondary Teachers,* and published articles. He can be reached at dave.nagel@corwin.com.

John Almarode, PhD, is an Associate Professor of Education at James Madison University who has held directorships with the Center for STEM Education Outreach and Engagement and the Content Teaching Academy. Prior to his work with schools, he served as a mathematics and science teacher in Virginia. John has engaged in professional learning with teachers and instructional leaders across the globe, integrating the science of how we learn into classrooms in all content areas and across all grade levels. He has published numerous books on teaching and learning, such as *Clarity for Learning* and *From Snorkelers to Scuba Divers*. He can be reached at almarojt@jmu.edu.

Douglas Fisher, PhD, is Professor of Educational Leadership at San Diego State University and a leader at Health Sciences High and Middle College. He has served as a teacher, language development specialist, and administrator in public schools and nonprofit organizations, including 8 years as the Director of Professional Development for the City Heights Collaborative, a time of increased student achievement in some of San Diego's urban schools. Doug has engaged in Professional Learning Communities for several decades, building teams that design and implement systems to impact teaching and learning. He has published numerous books on teaching and learning, such as *Developing Assessment-Capable Visible Learners* and *Engagement by Design*. He can be reached at dfisher@sdsu.edu.

Nancy Frey, PhD, is a Professor of Educational Leadership at San Diego State University and a leader at Health Sciences High and Middle College. She has been a special education teacher, reading specialist, and administrator in public schools. Nancy has engaged in Professional Learning Communities as a member and in designing schoolwide systems to improve teaching and learning for all students. She has published numerous books, including *The Teacher Clarity Playbook* and *Rigorous Reading*. She can be reached at nfrey@sdsu.edu.

Karen Flories, MS Ed, is a full-time Professional Learning Consultant for Corwin and works with teachers and leaders across the nation. Prior to her role with Corwin, Karen was the Executive Director of Educational Services and Director of Literacy and Social Studies in Valley View School District, after serving as the English Department Chair for Romeoville High School. Karen's classroom experience includes high school English, special education, and alternative education. She has co-authored several books, including student learner notebooks on *Becoming an Assessment-Capable Visible Learner* for Grades 3–5 and 6–12. She can be reached at karen.flories@corwin.com.

INTRODUCTION

Before we move into the work of an *activator*, let's look in on a sixth grade social studies PLC meeting. Although this particular team meets on a regular basis, today's extended planning meeting will be devoted to the analysis of its members' common formative assessment results. Over the past semester, a district-wide group of teachers devoted much time to developing these common assessments and making sure they align with the state standards in social studies. The common assessments place a heavy emphasis on the analysis of primary and secondary sources and/or text rather than the proficiency of learners in recalling and memorizing historical facts. Let's take a look at the conversation amongst the teachers in this team.

Mr. Vance:	I just cannot believe how *bad these assessment results are*. I mean, seriously, this isn't the first time our kids were ever asked to read and answer questions. We went over this again and again in class. Now what are we supposed to do with this? I'm not a reading teacher. *I don't know what to do about the reading problem. With all of the content we are expected to cover, I don't have time to teach reading.*
	Mr. Vance folds his arms and reclines back in his seat.
Mrs. Hearten:	I know. These results sure are rough to see. I can't believe we have so many Grade 6 students who still struggle so much with reading. I mean, look, most kids missed questions that required any type of synthesizing information from multiple sources. I mean w*hat happened in elementary school?*
	Mr. Vance unfolds his arms to grab his cell phone and begin scrolling.
Ms. Lee:	I wonder what Mrs. Leary [the principal] is going to think when *she* reviews these results. Do you think she'll come and have a talk with us? I don't see how we are going to have them ready by the end of the year. Plus, we have to move on.
	(Continued)

(Continued)

	Mr. Vance puts his cell phone down long enough to make a couple more comments.
Mr. Vance:	Do we have to put these in the grade book as a summative? So many of my students' grades are going to drop if this counts as a summative assessment. Then they won't be motivated to do anything from this point forward. Some of them just fail one thing after another. This is frustrating for both them and me.
Mr. Luis:	Team, I get it and I feel the same way, but I think we can focus on what's ahead of us. The common assessment is done. The results are what they are. Now we have to use them to make adjustments. These results prompt me to do something about the apparent gaps in learning. Where do we need to go next? I think we have three more post-assessments we have to administer before the school year ends. Let's talk about what we see in these results that we can act and build upon. For example, I noticed that many kids did well with items where they had to find information to support their choices. That wasn't the case first semester at all. Actually, let's look at the first semester results.

The team members all acknowledge with their facial expressions and mannerisms that he is right, and the tone of the meeting moves from what seemed to be contentious complaining into problem-solving mode.

As you read through the above scenario, you likely could relate to it or easily picture this exact conversation occurring during your PLC meeting. In fact, we have shared this scenario or similar ones with groups of teachers. Without exception, someone in the room asks, "Did you come watch our PLC meeting last week and record us . . . I mean except for the last statement by Mr. Luis?"

In a PLC+ meeting, all questions, anxieties, and perspectives are valued. Credibility and collective efficacy are rooted in the professional trust of the team. Mr. Vance, Mrs. Hearten, and Ms. Lee should not have their questions, anxieties, or perspectives squashed for the sole purpose of keeping the room "happy." When student growth and achievement is on the line, a certain level of anxiety is expected. A PLC+ can visit those anxieties, but it should not live there. The catalyst for moving this dialogue from defensiveness and avoidance to decisions and actions that improve teaching and learning is a person who can validate and still challenge, someone who can allow *venting* but prevent *lamenting*, and someone who can ensure a problem-solving and solution-based focus. We call these individuals *activators*. These are the members of the team that ensure the core value of activation is lived out consistently within the PLC+ team.

REFLECTION

Revisit the conversation amongst the members of the sixth grade social studies PLC. How would or have you contributed to the conversation? How would that contribution be similar to or different from that of Mr. Luis? In other words, which teacher are you in the above scenario? Use the Venn diagram to record your reflection.

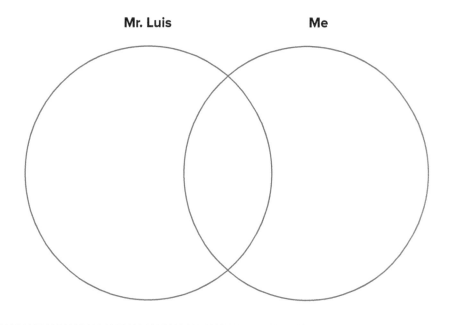

Mr. Luis   Me

Let's review. The five guiding questions of a PLC+ are a compass for teams to follow. As a refresher, here are those five questions:

1. Where are we going?

2. Where are we now?

3. How do we move learning forward?

4. What did we learn today?

5. Who benefited and who did not benefit?

See *The PLC+ Playbook* (Module 1, page 8) and *PLC+: Better Decisions and Greater Impact by Design* (pages 8 and 9).

Over the course of a school year, teams will engage in focused attention to all five of these questions, both in specific individual meetings and throughout the entire inquiry cycle. The PLC+ framework is steeped in the four crosscutting values. These values reflect the recent research on how to ensure that the diverse needs of all students are met by the teachers who serve them.

1. We must keep the **equity** of access and opportunity for learning at the forefront of each PLC+ collaborative team meeting.

See *The PLC+ Playbook* (Module 2, pages 13 and 14) and *PLC+: Better Decisions and Greater Impact by Design* (pages 9–11).

2. We must ensure that **activation** of the dialogue is provoked by the five questions and is carried out in such a way that the work of the PLC+ is accelerated, not hindered or impeded.

3. We must develop learning experiences that make our **expectations** for learning clear to all students.

4. And finally, the collaborative work of the PLC+ should leverage our **individual efficacy** into **collective teacher efficacy**.

REFLECTION

Using a dictionary, laptop, tablet, or other device, look up the word *activator*. Jot down the definitions of that word here. Just out of curiosity, and for our own professional learning, we also looked up the definition of an *activator*. In addition to the expected definition of a person or thing that activates, the word is defined on dictionary.com as a catalyst in biochemistry or chemistry and as an agent that renders another substance active or accelerates a process or reaction. But those three definitions are not even the most interesting ones. The definition that really stood out for us is "an impurity in a mineral that causes luminescence" (www.dictionary.com).

In the previous sentences, circle the words in the definitions of an *activator* that stand out to you. List them below in the first box, the box on the left:

WORDS	EXPLANATION

In the box on the right, explain why you circled those specific words. What about those words grabbed your attention?

Finally, as we have articulated in *PLC+: Better Decisions and Greater Impact by Design* and *The PLC+ Playbook, Grades K–12: A Hands-On Guide to Collectively Improving Student Learning* (Fisher, Frey, Almarode, Flories, & Nagel, 2020a, 2020b, Corwin) the **plus** in the PLC+ is *you*, the teacher. We, the teachers, have been missing in many PLC models. Each teacher brings a wide range of experiences, specific expertise, skills, understandings, and knowledge about teaching and learning that augments the sum of the parts in a PLC. Your contributions allow your PLC+ to be greater as a whole than any of us would be individually. We, collectively and collaboratively, focus on *both* teacher and student learning. This is part of what sets the PLC+ model apart from others, and it is also what provides the foundation for collaborative efforts that truly impact the learning of all students at the highest levels . . . not by chance but by design. We fully acknowledge that strong activation is a must for any PLC team to thrive.

Contained in the eight parts of this guide are concrete structures and actions *activators* and other team members can use to serve as a catalyst for your PLC+ meetings. As an *activator*, your role is as an agent that moves the substance of the dialogue actively toward effective teaching and learning; you accelerate that dialogue into action through the PLC+ framework. You may find, as did Mr. Luis in the sixth grade social studies PLC meeting, that you are alone in your perspective, maybe even considered an impurity in the PLC structure. However, as an *activator*, you have the role of shining a light on the wide range of experiences, specific expertise, skills, understandings, and knowledge about teaching and learning that are greater than the sum of the parts in a PLC. Remember, the *plus* is all about building capacity in our colleagues.

THE PATH FORWARD

This process is a journey. There are many challenges and obstacles PLC+ teams will face throughout their journey. Some of them are structural and are beyond the scope of influence or control of PLC+ team members. Two examples are the contractual time available to collaborate and how members of the PLC+ team are configured. This activator's guide and the other two books in this series cannot solve all of those challenges and obstacles. Other challenges are more affective and relational, and these are the challenges we will focus on in the eight parts of this book. These challenges include how the team

- Develops and utilizes norms and protocols
- Determines foci for its meetings (and what to do when these do not fit with all team members' desires)
- Engages in some of the hard conversations on topics such as race, equity, and other issues of justice and conscience

These are not easy conversations to have, as they often will shed light on some larger challenges our team is facing with the students its members serve. Yet these difficulties can be opportunities for our team to develop efficacy and thrive over time as we collectively address and overcome them. Without *activators*, these discussions will either not occur or, when they do, they may derail PLC+ teams, causing them to flounder at best or implode at worst. These hurdles and challenges provide opportunities for our PLC+ to overcome challenges and increase our collective efficacy as well as our self-efficacy.

HOW THE GUIDE IS DESIGNED

This activator's guide was designed to support PLC+ teams at all levels, specifically from the lens of the *activator*. While we believe the *activator* will be the individual leading the team, it's an important distinction within the PLC+ framework that *everyone* on the team can serve as the *activator* at certain times to ensure learning is moving forward for both the adults and our students. We are also aware that teams will engage in the PLC+ framework at different stages and have different needs based on their experience collaborating, the time and resources they have available, and so on, but we are all moving toward a common goal: an effective PLC+.

THE SIX CHARACTERISTICS OF A PLC

Background Work: Together, we will engage in an interactive exploration and analysis of the why, how, and what of PLC+ through the eyes of an *activator*.

1. Find Module 1, pages 5–7 in *The PLC+ Playbook*. As an *activator*, engage in a self-assessment about your current PLC.

2. Find the narrative in the core book that unpacks these characteristics (*PLC+: Better Decisions and Better Impact by Design*, pages 6–7). Use that section as an additional resource.

3. At this point in our journey, this should be an individual task. Later, as you begin your work with your PLC+, you might also engage in this task with your colleagues. However, for now, use it for yourself as foundational work for what comes next.

AN OVERVIEW OF THIS GUIDE

The following summary (Table I.1) provides an overview of each part of this guide so that you can use it as a flexible tool tailored to your particular situation.

TABLE I.1

OVERVIEW OF *THE PLC+ ACTIVATOR'S GUIDE*

Part 1. Activating Your PLC+: Overview Page 9	This part provides an overview of what it means to be an *activator*. What are some considerations of actions and behaviors for those who will be guiding their PLC+ teams?	• Activating Your PLC+
		 • What Effective *Activators* Do
		   ○ Activating Collaborative Maturity
		     □ Nine Ways to Build Collaborative Maturity
		   ○ Ensuring Fidelity to PLC+ Without Rigidity

Part 2. Activation Requires Effective Collaboration Page 23	Part 2 supports *activators* on a deep level in developing skills to foster, nurture, and sustain collaboration in their PLC+ meetings.	• Facilitation Versus Activation • Five Qualities of a Good *Activator* ○ Quality Activation Takes Practice: Establishing Habits for Consistency in PLC+ Meetings and Possible Scripts for *Activators*

(Continued)

TABLE I.1 (Continued)

Part 3. Activating Your PLC+: Establishing Roles and Developing Team Cohesion Page 33	Part 3 addresses the task of assigning roles and responsibilities for members of the PLC+ based on their strengths.	<ul><li>Supporting Team Cohesion</li><li>Establishing PLC+ Roles</li><li>Stepping Into Roles Matched to PLC+ Team Member Strengths<ul><li>Ensuring Clarity When Stepping Into Roles (Clarifying Tasks to Be Completed)</li></ul></li></ul>
Part 4. Activating Your PLC+: Norms and Authentic Instructional Protocols in Your PLC+ Page 49	Part 4 builds upon Part 3 and helps *activators* lead their PLC+ in developing authentic norms and protocols that become guides for structuring their PLC+ meetings.	<ul><li>Establishing Operating Norms</li><li>Social and Emotional Check-Ins</li><li>Establishing Process Norms</li><li>Operating Norms Versus Process Norms</li><li>Utilizing Authentic Instructional Protocols</li></ul>
Part 5. Activating the Five Essential Questions and Four Crosscutting Values Page 63	Part 5 provides structures for *activators* to lead PLC+ meetings specifically focused on the five guiding questions and four core values of the PLC+ framework.	<ul><li>Activating Guiding Questions: A Review of Each Guiding Question</li><li>Possible Challenges When Activating Each Question and Possible Responses:<ul><li>Suggestions for overcoming specific question-related challenges</li><li>Questions and sentence starters to guide the learning of the team</li><li>Specific suggestions for activating discussions on the PLC+ crosscutting values</li></ul></li></ul>
Part 6. The Nuts and Bolts of Your PLC+ Scheduling PLC+ Meetings and Meeting Cycles Page 95	Part 6 is devoted to providing examples of structures needed for a PLC+ to function on an ongoing basis in your school or district.	<ul><li>Example of a PLC+ Meeting Cycle<ul><li>Specific Meeting Descriptions</li><li>Sample Calendar and Schedules</li><li>Sample PLC+ Meeting Agendas</li></ul></li><li>Developing an Assessment Calendar<ul><li>Sample Assessment Calendar</li></ul></li></ul>
Part 7. Activating a High-Impact and High-Functioning PLC+ Page 119	How do you monitor your team's promotion of both student and adult learning? Part 7 will help you with this.	<ul><li>Differences Between High-Impact and High-Functioning Teams</li><li>Moving Toward a High-Impact and a High-Functioning Team</li><li>Navigating the Professional and Personal Dynamics of Your PLC+: Fourteen Common Problems and Solutions</li></ul>
Part 8. Activating Conversations Focused on Equity Page 143	Part 8 was designed to help support *activators* lead PLC+ teams in discussions related to race and equity with depth and dignity.	<ul><li>Glenn Singleton's Protocol With Four Guiding Considerations for Conversations About Equity</li><li>Sample *Activator*–Team Dialogues to Illustrate Singleton's Protocol</li></ul>

Part 1

ACTIVATING YOUR PLC+

Overview

Are you ready to *activate* your PLC+? Strong activation is essential for success in all PLC+ settings. PLC+ teams will face many challenges and ups and downs through the course of a school year. The role of the *activator* is critical to the success of the PLC+ framework in moving forward the learning of both the adults and the students the PLC+ team serves. Many previous PLC models and frameworks have disregarded the role human behavior plays when it comes to collaborative efforts to impact student learning at high levels. The PLC+ framework takes into account this critical element of human behavior on a deep level, with activation as one of its crosscutting values. *Activators* have the ability to move a PLC+ team from chaos and dysfunction into impactful action, from where team members are stagnant to where they are thriving. *Activators* ensure their teams' PLC+ journeys are focused on the learning and development of both adults and the students they teach. In doing so, *activators* arm their teams to weather the storms that will certainly come their way and to overcome any challenges they will face.

A CLOSE LOOK AT THE PLC+ VALUE OF ACTIVATION

Spotsylvania County Public Schools (SCPS) is the 12th-largest school division in the state of Virginia. SCPS consists of 29 schools and has an enrollment of approximately 24,000 students. It is a rural school system that rests between Washington, DC, and Richmond and has experienced significant changes in student demographics over the past 15 years. Like many school divisions in Virginia, SCPS has experienced state and federal sanctions for

(Continued)

(Continued)

underachieving schools due to an increase in rigor on state assessments and accountability revisions.

The core belief of SCPS is that *all* learners have the right to high-quality instruction, and PLC+ is the vehicle by which they will bring this core belief to actualization. Division Superintendent Dr. Scott Baker recognized the value of professional learning communities and, at the same time, noticed the immediate need to refocus the current approach to how these teams of educators operated within schools. Dr. Baker, drawing from firsthand experiences as an educator, building-level leader, and district-level leader, recognized that the best pathway to the success of PLCs was to embed this important initiative in classrooms and to entrust it to those doing the work in classrooms: the teacher. Dr. Baker believes that the *plus* is the teacher and the focus should be on the critical role teachers play in student learning for SCPS. By acknowledging that the *plus* is the teacher—*every* teacher in SCPS—Dr. Baker envisioned that the perception of "us," the teachers, and "they," the central office staff, would evolve into "we"—together, engaged in teaching and learning with intention and purpose, which is best for the learners in SCPS. Therefore, he made the decision to make this a district-wide focus, as well as the focus of his instructional leadership team.

The SCPS instructional leadership team, under the direction of Dr. Carol Flenard, Deputy Superintendent and Chief Academic Officer, determined that it would work to revitalize the division's PLCs district wide, as capacity-building vehicles that sustain change in teacher practice and thus student growth in learning and achievement. Members of the initiative began their journey by engaging in professional learning as an instructional leadership team. This required deep learning around the PLC+ framework, the four crosscutting values, and the deliberate, intentional, and purposeful analysis of each module in *The PLC+ Playbook*.

However, one afternoon during an instructional leadership meeting, the conversation about district-wide implementation came to a screeching halt. The implementation, excuse me, the *successful* implementation of PLC+ in a district with 29 different locations required meticulous and diligent identification and support of the initial *activators* to serve as the catalyst for implementing PLC+ across the district, rendering action or accelerating this revitalization of the PLCs of SCPS. Without this catalyst or the initial *activators* embracing this particular crosscutting value of *activation*, the PLC+ would likely spiral into "another meeting." We will check in with the work of this particular school district as we progress through the other parts of this guide for *activators*. However, the recognition of the importance of identifying and supporting *activators* brings us to the first part of this guide. What makes an *activator* effective?

10   The PLC+ Activator's Guide

ACTIVATING YOUR PLC+

Background Work: At the conclusion of Chapters 2, 3, 4, 5, and 6 in *PLC+: Better Decisions and Greater Impact by Design*, there is a table that summarizes how each of the four crosscutting values is reflected in the specific PLC+ question addressed in that chapter. To begin our close-up look at what constitutes effective activation, visit the section devoted to the *activator* in each chapter (see below). On the form on page 13, begin to synthesize the information into what an *activator* is or is not. You may wish to revisit the chapter for key takeaways. Use the chart that follows to organize your thinking.

Question 1: *Where Are We Going?* Activation

PLC+: BETTER DECISIONS AND GREATER IMPACT BY DESIGN, PAGE 55

ACTIVATION	Keeping a PLC+ focused on what students need to know rather than what is neat to know requires an *activator*. Teams can digress very easily when determining what all students must be expected to learn. Getting off topic stifles the efficiency of the PLC+ and takes away their ability to keenly focus on what students need to learn, as well as on the evidence that will demonstrate they have done so.

- How do you currently employ facilitation strategies in your PLC+ structure?
- What strengths does your PLC+ have around facilitation?
- What opportunities does your PLC+ have around facilitation?
- What facilitation strategies does your PLC+ use to determine whether all members understand "where are we going?"
- What opportunities does your PLC+ provide to build content knowledge?

Question 2: *Where Are We Now?* Activation

PLC+: BETTER DECISIONS AND GREATER IMPACT BY DESIGN, PAGE 83

ACTIVATION	There is a lot of "noise" in the world of teachers. *Activators* help keep the PLC+ conversations focused, productive, and objective. Teachers don't ever talk about having too much time on their hands, and effective activation supports efficiency within the PLC+ so that there is time to be action oriented in response to the challenges the team identifies.

- Which initial assessments are useful to determine what students already know?
- How can you activate hard conversations about data?
- How do you keep the team focused on the data review rather than hypothesizing solutions?

Question 3: *How Do We Move Learning Forward?* Activation

PLC+: BETTER DECISIONS AND GREATER IMPACT BY DESIGN, PAGE 115

ACTIVATION

As you have seen in this chapter, teachers have access to numerous instructional strategies so that student learning continuously moves forward. It is important to ensure that strategies selected are evidence based and appropriate for the learning needs of your students. Many teachers use strategies without knowledge of the research behind them or the impact they can potentially have on student learning.

- When discussing different strategies in your PLC+ to use in the classroom, what would be an important role of the *activator*?
- How might the PLC+ facilitate dialogue around the validity of the selection of specific strategies?
- In what ways can the *activator* ensure that all voices in the PLC+ are heard when thinking about strategies that will move learning forward?

Question 4: *What Did We Learn Today?* Activation

PLC+: BETTER DECISIONS AND GREATER IMPACT BY DESIGN, PAGE 143

ACTIVATION

Effectively analyzing student performance data within a PLC+ can often be a challenge. There will always be one teacher whose data are the highest and one whose are lowest. The critical factor is to look at the data in terms of *impact*. PLC+ teams need to constantly engage in discourse around the learning tasks they engineered, the strategies they used to support students in engaging in those tasks, and, as a result, how well students performed against the established learning intentions.

- What do you think are key attributes of an *activator* who can facilitate a PLC+ discussion where teachers can allow themselves to be vulnerable?
- What is the link between effective facilitation and genuine reflection?
- How can the *activator* create an environment of trust so that people can talk honestly about the data?

Question 5: *Who Benefitted and Who Did Not Benefit?* Activation

PLC+: BETTER DECISIONS AND GREATER IMPACT BY DESIGN, PAGE 176

ACTIVATION

As we have said before, effectively analyzing student performance data within a PLC+ can often be a challenge. Looking at who did and did not benefit makes this all the more challenging. When we look at the growth versus achievement grid through the lens of impact, we must work collaboratively to ensure that our conversations are focused on what to do about those learners not benefiting from instruction. Strong activation of such challenging conversations is paramount.

- What do you think are key attributes of an *activator* who can facilitate a PLC+ discussion where teachers can allow themselves to be vulnerable?
- What is the link between effective activation and genuine reflection?

TABLE 1.1

KEY TAKEAWAYS FOR ACTIVATORS

PLC+ GUIDING QUESTION	SUMMARY OF THE ACTIVATOR ROLE	KEY TAKEAWAYS
Chapter 2: Where are we going? (page 55)		
Chapter 3: Where are we now? (page 83)		
Chapter 4: How do we move learning forward? (page 115)		
Chapter 5: What did we learn today? (page 143)		
Chapter 6: Who benefited and who did not? (page 176)		

Having a clear understanding and thus a clear picture of an *activator* in PLC+ allows us to begin reflecting on three key questions.

At this point in your journey, what are your answers to the three questions below? Write them in the boxes, and then mark this page in the guide. We will return to these questions as we move through the other parts of the *activator's* guide.

THREE KEY QUESTIONS

What does my role as an *activator* look like while doing the work of PLC+?

What professional learning do I need to step into that role?

How will I use this role and my own professional learning as catalysts for accelerating my colleagues into *activators*?

WHAT EFFECTIVE ACTIVATORS DO

Effective PLC+ *activators*

1. Have high credibility with their colleagues and students

2. Can lead adults in *their* learning process

3. Have the ability to effectively challenge the team members, their colleagues, and themselves

4. Truly believe all students and all teachers can learn at high levels

5. Demonstrate resilience in times of challenge

What's more important than what *activators* are is how they leverage that identity to accomplish the goals of the PLC+. Your actions will have a tremendous impact on your PLC+'s success and on the learning of your PLC+ team members. That will in turn impact the learning of students the team members serve. Two essential things *all activators* must do and do well are

- *Activate collaborative maturity*

- *Ensure fidelity to* (but not the rigidity of) *the PLC+ process*

ACTIVATING COLLABORATIVE MATURITY

We all believe in the professionalism of teaching, and this belief must be lived out at all times, by every educator, every day. We are professionals and thus the behavior in PLC+ meetings must be professional. There is nothing wrong with being friendly and keeping the mood light, but there needs to be a professional atmosphere in every PLC+ meeting. That isn't always easy. Sometimes this is because team members don't get along or don't fully respect the other adults on the team. A disrespectful or unfriendly atmosphere is a challenge some of you will face as *activators*. Also challenging for *activators* are PLC+ members who are *too friendly*. Then the bigger issue becomes how to keep team members from being so relaxed together that they get off task and talk more about an upcoming social gathering than about what's on the meeting's agenda. The struggle in this situation is to focus on the current task at hand. Meetings can become places where conversations are more like those at a cocktail party—and about everything *except* teaching and learning.

When team members are very friendly, another challenge can arise: team members may be unwilling to be fully honest. They may avoid healthy but challenging dialogue about teaching and learning. Hard conversations are necessary in a well-functioning PLC+. But if no one is willing to challenge practices, PLC meetings can become simply a "land of nice."

> The most striking result is the negative correlation between student achievement and "friendship" interactions among teachers—the more

friendship interactions, the lower students' academic achievement. . . . [These] findings based on correlations . . . do cast doubt on the perception that teachers must be friends or engage in social interactions for the school to be effective. (Marzano, 2003, pp. 61–62)

As *activators*, you set the tone for all PLC+ meetings, and in doing so, you develop credibility with your peers.

REFLECTION

How would you describe the level of collaborative maturity in your PLC or your PLC+? Why do you believe that? What role do you play in setting the level of collaborative maturity in the PLC or PLC+? Use the space below to jot down your thoughts.

_____

_____

_____

_____

_____

_____

_____

_____

_____

_____

_____

_____

_____

_____

_____

_____

_____

Be the Catalyst: Let's look inside the playbook of a PLC+ *activator*. Using *The PLC+ Playbook*, identify modules that would specifically support you as an *activator*. List them in the chart below. In the second column, brainstorm how you would use the modules to serve as a catalyst for your PLC+ team and build capacity in your colleagues. Be specific. Plan out what you would say and do.

MODULE	HOW WOULD I USE THIS MODULE?
Module _____ Page_____	
Module _____ Page_____	
Module _____ Page_____	
Module _____ Page_____	
Module _____ Page_____	
Module _____ Page_____	

In addition to the specific modules in *The PLC+ Playbook,* there are other ways to promote collaborative maturity. Below are nine things to consider.

NINE WAYS TO BUILD COLLABORATIVE MATURITY

1. **Be prepared:** The team will follow your lead. If you are prepared and ready to lead the meeting, the chances your peers will be invested immediately increase dramatically. For example, the summary activity in Table 1.1 will help prepare you to activate the four PLC+ crosscutting values. As you and your PLC+ move forward, delegating that preparation list will help build capacity within the team.

2. **Provide a time for people to let it out:** Teachers need time to vent, share personal issues, and talk about their day. Sometimes their PLC meeting is the only time they get to talk with adults. A simple strategy? Allow five minutes at the beginning of the meeting for team members to share happenings in their lives. It's important to set an external timer so there is an indicator when the five minutes are up and to signal that it's now time to get to business.

3. **Establish routines and authentically stick to them:** Maintain a professional tone at all times during the meeting. Refer back to your team's establishment of norms in *The PLC+ Playbook*. This will help remind members that they are all part of the PLC+ team and collectively invested in the norms you created together.

4. **Share leadership and ownership of meetings:** Provide time for other members to be responsible for making the meeting a success. Prior to each PLC+ meeting, give members the opportunity to help prepare for the meeting. Give them a list of choices based on the preparation needed. One strategy: develop a to-do list prior to the conclusion of each meeting. Then, sign your name next to items that you have already begun, and encourage others to sign up for the rest.

5. **Be the catalyst:** Using your background work from the beginning of this chapter, start developing a list of tasks or items that need to be done before the start of each meeting. Organize this list in categories by the five guiding questions. Put this list online for your PLC+ team members to see and access.

6. **Being businesslike doesn't mean being stuffy:** Have a sense of humor, and make sure there are times when the meeting is fun; it's important and allows the team to let off steam. Building efficacy requires the recognition and celebration of successes within the group. Take time to use the data and evidence generated by the five guiding questions to feed the individual and collective belief that we can and do have an impact on student learning.

7. **Be comfortable with wait time:** The initial *activator* often tries to do everything, to provide answers and solutions to every challenge that comes up in the PLC+. Be comfortable utilizing wait time when the team is digging into important questions and issues during PLC+ dialogue. This will require practice. Letting the conversation, or silence, occur may be the process needed at that moment. If the conversation or silence begins to lead toward an issue not related to teaching and learning, that is the time to render action by returning to the routines (see #3 in this list) or to modules in *The PLC+ Playbook*. However, being able to nudge the group back toward these requires that, as *activators*, we are familiar with the modules prior to the PLC+ meeting.

8. **Be a servant leader:** Do more than others can ever expect of you. As the initial *activator*, be prepared to let your own commitment to the process do the "talking." Early on, you may have to add a few more items to your own to-do list that include developing a high level of comfort and familiarity with the protocols. Helping you achieve this knowledge was the purpose behind the previously listed "Be the Catalyst" task.

9. **Take your job, not yourself, seriously**: Be willing more than anyone else on the team to be humble, acknowledge mistakes, and ensure team members see you as an *activator* of *their* team and a *member* of the team as well at all times. The *activator* should be willing to put his or her data out for discussion first, using a personal reflective think aloud as a model.

See *The PLC+ Playbook* (Module 3, page 19) and *PLC+: Better Decisions and Greater Impact by Design* (pages 15–17).

What the above nine items have in common is that communication is key in the success of the meeting. Communicate before, during, and after meetings. This communication should be clear, concise, and transparent.

REFLECTION

Using Module 3 from *The PLC+ Playbook* and pages 15–17 in the core book, develop a list of things you can do to enhance credibility with your colleagues. Be specific. In fact, you may want to work through "Your Individual Identity" (on page 20 of Module 3) before moving to "Teacher Credibility" (on pages 21–24 of the same module).

_____

_____

_____

_____

_____

_____

_____

_____

_____

_____

_____

_____

_____

_____

ENSURING FIDELITY TO PLC+ WITHOUT RIGIDITY

A critical task *activators* must do is to ensure that their PLC+ *is a PLC+*. PLCs are not static; they grow and develop over time as a reflection of the answers to each of the five guiding questions, as well as according to the evolution of the crosscutting values. Increased efficacy, the assurance of equity, and the professional growth of colleagues into *activators* sets up our schools and classrooms to be dynamic, innovative, and progressive learning spaces. As *activators*, we must help the PLC+ develop a structure that is malleable, adjusting for the many nuances and natural interwoven elements a group of diverse educators brings to the table. Successful implementation of any professional learning in a school requires *adaptation*. Penuel, Phillips, and Harris (2014) examined educational research related to the implementation of programs in schools to help determine which stages of implementation could inform development and improve practice. One of their core findings was the need for adaptations at what they called the "local contexts" (p. 752). In an earlier paper, Penuel, Frank, Fishman, Sabelli, and Cheng (2009) cite McDonald (2009), who noted that if programs could not adapt to a range of contexts and be usable in those contexts, implementation of those programs might falter and negatively impact outcomes. In this case, the program is similar to the work of the PLC+. *Activators* make sure that the structure they provide their PLC+ team is like the structure provided in a classroom in which they teach, a structure with clearly defined cognitive, social, and emotional learning outcomes but with multiple pathways toward those outcomes. To take this a step further, *activators* recognize when adaptive approaches are needed to carry out the work of the PLC+.

Penuel and his colleagues (2009) also cited evidence that teachers' adaptations of any program are congruent with designers' intentions, seeking to distinguish "creative transformations" from "lethal mutations" in teachers' enactments (A.L. Brown & Campione, 1996; M.W. Brown & Edelson, 2001). They went on to say that poor implementation can diminish the potential impact and strength of any program, making it less likely to point to how the program led to positive impacts on student learning (Cordray & Pion, 2006).

As *activators*, we must ensure that the focus of the team's efforts and actions stays within the confines of a true PLC+. There is intentionality in how the PLC+ framework was developed. Skipping questions or cherry-picking values would, for example, not be true to the model and could lead to outcomes that were never intended during this work. As a specific example, working through the guiding question "Where are we now?" before working through the guiding question "Where are we going?" will lead to low expectations. If we first focus on where are learners are now, we are likely to then set expectations that are biased toward that starting point. Phrases such as "Well, that is about as much as they can handle" or "They can't do that" permeate the conversation space. These low expectations tip the equity scale out of balance, lowering the efficacy of the individual teachers and thus the collective efficacy of the PLC+ team. Again, there is intentionality in how the PLC+ framework was developed.

A "lethal adaptation" cannot happen if the team understands clearly and uses all of the guiding questions and crosscutting values. As *activator*, you ensure the model in its entirety is used as intended; you use this structure to shape and form the dialogue, discussions, and decisions the team generates collectively. *Activators* make sure the sidelines and boundaries for the team are clear.

Be the Catalyst: Using your response to the above reflection on teacher credibility, list the adaptations you believe are necessary for your local context. Then, outline the steps you will take as the *activator* to make those adaptions. Keep in mind that these adaptions may be opportunities to provide time for other members to be responsible for making the meeting a success (see on page 18 of this guide the fourth item in the list of the ways to build collaborative maturity).

_____

_____

_____

_____

_____

_____

_____

_____

_____

_____

_____

_____

_____

_____

_____

_____

_____

_____

_____

_____

_____

_____

NOTES

Part 2

ACTIVATION REQUIRES EFFECTIVE COLLABORATION

FACILITATION VERSUS ACTIVATION

Activation is much more than facilitation. Facilitating a meeting suggests a hierarchy and places the responsibility on a single individual. Whether intentional or not, this situation opens the door for divesting other PLC+ members of ownership. Instead, leveraging the wide range of experiences, specific expertise, skills, understandings, and knowledge about teaching and learning leads to a high functioning PLC+ team. You will not find a high functioning PLC+ team, one driving the learning of its members and the learning of their students to high levels, that has meetings facilitated by an appointed or nominated facilitator. Activation is fundamentally different: as an *activator*, you are essential in making sure your group is successful and avoids or resolves many of the challenges and pitfalls a PLC team will face during a given school year. But having a plan to manage collaboratively the structural elements of your PLC+ is very important. As a point worth making, this will be the last time you see us using any form of the word facilitate. We suggest you purge that word from your PLC+ work as well. Let's look at why this word choice is so important.

A CLOSE LOOK AT EFFECTIVE COLLABORATION

This part of the activator's guide provides concrete strategies and tools to support individuals charged in *activating* the PLC+ team while addressing many complexities that make up schools from a technical and structural perspective.

A CLOSE LOOK AT IDENTIFYING AND SUPPORTING ACTIVATORS

Let's return to Spotsylvania County Public Schools and eavesdrop in on conversations about the identification and support of *activators*. In addition to directors, instructional coordinators, and building administrators, the superintendent and deputy superintendent were in the conference room, the location of the work session for implementing PLC+ district wide. Given the specific individuals in the room and their titles, a logical inference would be that the superintendent and the deputy superintendent were going to guide and direct the meeting. Furthermore, a safe assumption would be that both of these individuals would outline their perspectives on who would and would not be an *activator* and the steps for implementation. Instead, something remarkable was revealed in that conference. The room was occupied by *activators* who began a productive collaboration.

Each individual in the conference room possessed the characteristics of an *activator* and engaged in dialogue that transformed the meeting into a PLC+ team meeting. From directors to building administrators, each individual displayed clarity, consciousness, competence, confidence, and credibility in articulating where they wanted to go with PLC+, where they were now, how they would move the work forward, what measures would let them know how the work was going, and ways to support those that were not benefiting from the process. After much back and forth, excellent wait time, and careful examination of their local context, Darnella Cunningham, Director of Teaching and Learning said, "We need PLC+ teams to be able to do this." And she was right. How do we transform colleagues into rooms full of *activators* that serve as a catalyst for a process that maximizes teaching and learning: the essence of PLC+?

SCPS is fortunate in that its members experienced the role of an *activator* and were able to recognize it. Dr. Flenard and her superintendent, Dr. Baker, have long served as the initial *activators* of the PLC—the instructional leadership team. However, their role as *activators* led directly to building capacity within each member of their team such that, over time, all members now recognize activation points in the work they do in Spotsylvania County.

Looking back at your earlier work, let's synthesize your own professional learning. Using the space provided, list the qualities of a good _activator_. Using a marker or highlighter, <u>underline</u> those qualities you already have. Put a |square| around those that you believe are areas of growth for you. (Circle) those qualities about which you are unclear as to how they make a good _activator_. Reflect on those that you circled, how might they make a good _activator_.

_____

_____

_____

_____

_____

_____

_____

_____

_____

_____

_____

ALL ACTIVATORS ARE GREAT COLLABORATORS, BUT NOT ALL COLLABORATORS ARE ACTIVATORS BY DEFAULT!

Activators need to be strong collaborators above all else because they are charged with supporting, leading, and guiding the learning of a group of their fellow teachers. Going rogue or overlooking the need to collaborate perpetuates the negative practice of sitting through PLC+ meetings only to return to your own classroom where you close the door and do what you were going to do from the start. _Activators_ need to be able to foster, nurture, and sustain a PLC+ environment that allows teachers the time to work together. This starts with establishing the right mind frame for learning. _Activators_ must be able to provide the structure and environment that colleagues need, so all can create a forum for collaborative and productive struggle.

We can think of individuals who are collaborative in their work and have no problem working with others but seem to be missing the skills to render _action_ when the group needs that catalyst. Let's look at how we can be a collaborator _and_ _activator_.

See _The PLC+_
Playbook (page 53).

Be the Catalyst: Throughout *The PLC+ Playbook*, there are modules that direct you and your PLC+'s attention to the intersection of the crosscutting values and each of the five guiding questions. For example, on page 53, you are encouraged to use the "Activate Learning for Myself and Others Checklist" while considering the first guiding question. Look beyond page 53 to find all of the tasks that are associated with *activation* in the modules for each of the guiding questions. There should be a total of five tasks associated with the crosscutting value of *activation,* one for each question. Using the chart on the opposite page to organize your thoughts, reflect on the collaborative nature of each task or how the task promotes collaboration.

NOTES

TABLE 2.1

ACTIVATING COLLABORATION

THE PLAYBOOK MODULE TASK	CIRCLE/HIGHLIGHT THE WORDS OR PHRASES IN EACH TASK THAT PROMOTE COLLABORATION. THEN, LIST THOSE WORDS AND PHRASES HERE.	HOW DOES THIS TASK BUILD YOUR CAPACITY AS AN ACTIVATOR?	HOW WILL YOU USE THE TASK TO BUILD UP YOUR COLLEAGUES AS ACTIVATORS?
Example Activate Learning for Myself and Others, page 53			

FIVE QUALITIES OF A GOOD ACTIVATOR

Just like you have C's that describe 21st Century Learners, Garmston and Wellman (2009) identify specific qualities necessary for effective team collaboration that they refer to as **the five C's**: clarity, consciousness, competence, confidence, and credibility. These qualities are necessary for a strong *activator* as well. Table 2.2 describes each in detail and provides some examples of what this can look like when activated. Please read though the overview of each, listing any ideas you have for yourself as an *activator* in your PLC+, and then complete the "Five C's Reflection" in Table 2.3 on page 30.

TABLE 2.2

WAYS TO USE THE FIVE C'S IN YOUR PLC+

QUALITY	ELEMENT	EXAMPLES	WAYS TO USE THIS IN YOUR PLC+
Clarity	Uses precise language to minimize ambiguity and limit unnecessary frustration	"Our focus today is on supporting our common challenge, which is making sure our students have a strong grasp of stoichiometry. Bill, can you share two strategies you have used in the past that have worked for you?" "From analyzing our standard, we know that our students need to know . . . and be able to do . . ."	
Consciousness	Aware of human elements being conveyed such as body language, voice inflection, disengagement	"Joan, I notice you disagree with what we just shared. Can you share some of your thoughts?" "Okay, I can see we are getting a bit tired. Let's set the timer and take a five-minute stretch break to reenergize for the second half of our meeting."	

QUALITY	ELEMENT	EXAMPLES	WAYS TO USE THIS IN YOUR PLC+
Competence	Works at the craft of activation. Understands how to use types of conversation at the right time. Knows when to push and when to pull	"I see we are all sharing ideas at the same time. Let's divide and conquer. Bill, Steve, Karen, and Marc, would you go to that side of the room and come up with two or three strategies you think would move learning forward for our students? Sam, Bill, and I will do the same. Let's plan for 10 minutes and then come back together."	
Confidence	Has a strong sense of self-efficacy and believes in ability to help the team accomplish goals and overcome obstacles together	"I know we have some great strategies we all have used before, and if we work together, we can help our students grow. Can I share something I read about and tried last week to get some of your feedback?"	
Credibility	Earns this over time through being honest, neutral, trustworthy, fair, and willing to acknowledge personal mistakes	"So, I wanted to share three of my biggest learning opportunities from last week and what I learned from them." "Would everyone be willing to share at least one instance of learning from a challenge last week to see how we've collectively grown from our work?"	

Source: Adapted from Garmston R., & Wellman B. (2009). *The adaptive school: A sourcebook for developing collaborative groups* (2nd ed.). Lanham, MD: Rowman & Littlefield.

TABLE 2.3

FIVE C'S REFLECTION

REFLECTIVE QUESTIONS	THOUGHTS . . .
Revisit the reflection at the beginning of this part (page 25). How has your description of a good *activator* changed? What, specifically, changed your thinking?	
Which of the five C's do you possess naturally, and which are you ready to use in your role as an *activator*?	
Which of the qualities in your description of a good *activator* present an area for potential growth for you in your role as an *activator*? Which of the five C's present an area for potential growth in your role as an *activator*?	

QUALITY ACTIVATION TAKES PRACTICE

Many of you who are called to be *activators* will have a knack for working collaboratively with your PLC+. But becoming great takes time, practice, and the development of relationships that happen at every PLC+ meeting. Development of any skill requires sustained practice and feedback. Walking into a room full of colleagues whose learning you are expected to activate and ensuring that the team members collaborate with each other effectively takes more than good instincts; it takes thought and planning. The tasks within this part of the activator's guide are designed to promote your familiarity and comfort with the nature of activation through collaboration. For example, developing and practicing a script for communicating about clarity and the other C's will help you feel more comfortable and confident in your upcoming conversations.

Activators need to practice reflecting on patterns of their own behavior to then be able to engage effectively with others. Reflecting on patterns of your own behavior may seem hard at first, but like any other skills we work to develop, we get better simply by practicing. When we establish credibility, build our own individual efficacy, and contribute to the collective efficacy of the PLC+, the process becomes a natural part of how we do business. Effective teaching and learning become synonymous with the collaborative dialogue of our PLC+. This, in turn, allows for us to engage naturally in the difficult conversations because of the PLC+ team's level of credibility and efficacy.

Table 2.4 provides some concrete examples or possible scripts that activators might use for common routines in their PLC+ meetings.

TABLE 2.4

DEVELOPING SCRIPTS FOR ACTIVATORS

ESSENTIAL ACTIVATOR ROUTINES	SAMPLE SCRIPTS	YOUR SCRIPT
Opening the PLC+ Meeting	"Good morning! Today we get to dive into our data from Friday's common formative assessment. Let's see how we did with our instruction. Rachel, you put together the data and came up with our thinking questions for today. So, take it away."	
Establishing Norms	"Thank you, Rachel, it seems you found several trends in the data. This might be a tough conversation, so I have to remind myself of our norms, especially given my data and my need for feedback."	
Framing the Goal(s) for the Team	"Given our results, let's make sure we are clear on our learning outcomes, specifically in the area of reading comprehension with grade-level texts. What that means for us today is that we examine strategies to help our learners (1) make quality inferences from text and (2) cite the evidence. Last week, based on assessment results, we set a plan to move from 60 percent of our students able to do both tasks to 80 percent."	
Checking for Understanding	"We have agreed on using reciprocal teaching three times per week in our reading blocks for the next month. Do we all agree on what that needs to look like? Bill and Sam, can you please share what that will look like in your classroom?"	
Keeping Only One Process Happening at a Time	"Team, while we analyze the priority standards for this unit, we have to keep the focus solely there for the next 15 minutes, agreed?"	

(Continued)

TABLE 2.4 (Continued)

ESSENTIAL ACTIVATOR ROUTINES	SAMPLE SCRIPTS	YOUR SCRIPT
Maintaining Focus on Only One Topic at a Time	"I hear your concerns about the assessment. Let's put that in the parking lot. We are focused right now on question #3: 'How do we move learning forward?' For the next chunk of time, we need to stay focused on specific strategies we will agree to use and implement, agreed?"	
Using Precise Language to Elicit Specific Language Back	"Bill, you shared that you disagreed with where our students are in their ability to cite evidence. Can you share specifically what you mean with two or three examples?"	
Mediating Conflict	"Okay, Steve and Dawn, you obviously disagree on what learning progressions seem to be tripping the students up the most. You both have made valid points. Can we hear from others in the group? What do you think about this issue? Any other perspectives out there?"	
Testing for Consensus	"Okay, so we seem to have about five or six quality ideas for how to support some of our struggling learners. We need to pare that down to two or three at the most. Let's go around the table once and share which idea each of us thinks will work best for all of our students with this learning gap?"	
Intervening When Events Are Starting to Sidetrack the Team	"Okay, we have gotten off track. The points we are making are good, but we've lost focus. Let's reset for a moment. Bill, please reset the timer for 10 minutes, and let's stay focused on question #2, 'Where are we now?' Shall we?"	
Closing the Meeting Appropriately	"Team, that was a very productive meeting. We didn't finish everything on the agenda, but some really good learning took place. Bill, could you please recap with the summary and our next steps."	

Part 3

ACTIVATING YOUR PLC+

Establishing Roles and Developing Team Cohesion

You are not in this work alone. Although you may find yourself in the role of an *activator*, we do not mean to imply that you alone are now carrying the weight of your PLC+ on your shoulders. Yes, we make it very clear that *activators* **do not need to be building or district administrators.** However, that does not mean that *activators* take on the role as administrators of the PLC+. The PLC+ framework, through the five guiding questions immersed in the four crosscutting values, provides an environment where we as teachers can collaborate because of common attitudes, interests, and goals in teaching and learning. When our PLC+ grows into a cohesive team, each member takes ownership in the work. This common ownership is fueled by evidence of the impact and collective efficacy of the team. *Activators* work to build this common ownership by ensuring each member has a valued role in the work that results in a cohesive PLC+. To promote cohesion in your PLC+ and establish roles that build on individual strengths will require a clear focus on both the outcomes of the PLC+ and the assets available through the individual strengths of the members, as well as engaging in actions that move the dialogue forward.

A CLOSE LOOK AT A COHESIVE TEAM

Let us return once more to Spotsylvania County Public Schools and the district's cohesive instructional leadership team. To make meaning of the ease with which each member of Dr. Baker and Dr. Flenard's team owned her or his role within the leadership team and took common ownership of the work of the team, let's look at research on what makes an organization of professionals thrive. Dave Logan, John King, and Halee Fischer-Wright (2011) collected over 10 years of research across 24,000 people in their quest to understand what allowed some organizations to thrive while others fizzled out or even

(Continued)

(Continued)

crashed and burned. Excuse the harsh metaphor, but you see our point, right? Are there commonalities among teams of people, in our case a PLC+, that contribute to and almost guarantee success? As it turns out, they uncovered the idea that thriving organizations share the following commonalities:

1. They have an identified and agreed upon set of core values.

2. They leverage those core values in the direction of a noble cause.

3. They identify clear outcomes that will have a significant impact.

4. They recognize and acknowledge assets within the organization.

5. They map out a plan for "what to do."

Through the establishment of roles and the development of team cohesion in SCPS's instructional leadership team, each member builds his or her capacity in not only agreeing upon a set of core values, but owning his or her role in leveraging those values in the direction of a noble cause. Dr. Flenard describes this as "carrying the torch" and moving forward with "what to do." This allows for Dr. Baker to step back and truly let the assets within the team make the significant impact, quality instruction for all learners. This same process will likely occur in your district or school—the administrator may light the flame, but your job as an *activator* is to carry the torch, while at the same time building capacity in your PLC+ so that you do not have to carry the torch alone.

As you move forward in this guide, you will see that, as an *activator*, you will work to build capacity in your colleagues so that each one becomes an *activator*.

REFLECTION

In the table on the opposite page, take a few moments and map the work of Logan, King, and Fischer-Wright (2011) onto PLC+. How does the work of these scholars shed light on our task of establishing roles and developing team cohesion?

_____

_____

_____

_____

_____

_____

TABLE 3.1

FIVE COMMONALITIES OF COHESIVE TEAMS

CONCEPT	RELATIONSHIP TO PLC+	HOW THIS SUPPORTS MY WORK AS AN ACTIVATOR
Agreed Upon Set of Core Values		
Leverage Toward a Noble Cause		
Clear Outcomes of Significant Impact		
Recognize and Acknowledge Assets		
Plan for "What to Do"		

In Spotsylvania County Public Schools the instructional leadership team operates on the core values articulated in the district's "Framework for Teaching and Learning." This document articulates, in significant detail, the values of the school division and beliefs about teaching and learning. In addition, the team has agreed upon the four crosscutting values of PLC+: equity, expectations, individual and collective efficacy, and activation. These core values are leveraged toward the noble cause of preparing students for their future. A more immediate noble cause is the implementation of PLC+ so that, "together, we can amplify our impact in teaching and learning."

As you have likely noticed, the instructional leadership team *is* a PLC+. Members devoted an entire day to the articulation of clear outcomes with the implementation of PLC+, creating measurable goals at multiple points over the next three years. However, what makes this such a cohesive team is Dr. Baker and Dr. Flenard's heightened awareness of the team's assets. They recognize and acknowledge the individual strengths in the room, thus setting the team up for each member to take on tasks that leverage those strengths. So, when the time comes to make a plan for "what to do," individuals feel empowered to step up and assume roles that align with their recognized and acknowledged assets.

See *The PLC+ Playbook* (Module 3, page 20).

As *activators*, we must do the same thing in our PLC+. This part of the activator's guide provides tools to support the recognition and acknowledgement of the wide range of experiences, specific expertise, skills, understandings, and knowledge about teaching and learning and leverage these assets to establish roles within the work of the PLC+.

REFLECTION

Revisit Module 3 in *The PLC+ Playbook*. Before engaging in the collaborative work of your PLC+, make sure you have completed the section on "Your Individual Identity." How do the responses to each question around the *plus* symbol help you recognize and acknowledge the assets *you* bring to the PLC+? Use the table below to organize your thinking. In addition, develop a way to use this specific task in Module 3 to help your colleagues recognize and acknowledge the assets *they* bring to the PLC+.

TABLE 3.2

ESTABLISH IDENTITY AS AN EDUCATOR

INDIVIDUAL IDENTITY QUESTIONS	RECOGNIZED AND ACKNOWLEDGED ASSETS	WAYS TO USE ASSETS TO FURTHER TASKS OF PLC+
Why did you become an educator?		
What makes you a great teacher?		
What is your hope for your students?		
What goals do you have for yourself as an educator?		

Be the Catalyst: With your colleagues, plan for the implementation of your idea regarding the use of Module 3 which you generated in the previous reflection. Use the space provided to develop detailed steps for implementing the task. What will you say? Develop your script. How will you set the room up? Be specific.

_____

_____

_____

_____

_____

_____

_____

_____

_____

_____

_____

_____

_____

_____

_____

_____

_____

_____

_____

_____

_____

_____

_____

_____

_____

SUPPORTING TEAM COHESION

As we pointed out at the beginning of this part of the guide, research on cohesive teams suggests the need for five different things. Recall them and fill in the missing information here using terminology linked to PLC+.

1. They have an identified and agreed upon _____.

2. They leverage those _____ _____ in the direction of a _____ cause.

3. They identify clear _____ that will have a significant impact.

4. They recognize and acknowledge _____.

5. They map out a _____.

Specific modules in *The PLC+ Playbook* can help *activators* create meaning related to the five commonalities of effective teams introduced in this chapter and, at the same time, support that cohesion amongst colleagues. At this point in our journey, we should be very familiar with these protocols and be prepared to implement them to render action in our PLC+.

> **Be the Catalyst:** The chart below directly correlates these five commonalities with protocols in *The PLC+ Playbook*. We suggest that you pause in your reading and devote time to understanding each protocol and to developing an approach for implementing the protocol in your PLC+. As always, this implementation should build team cohesion through collaboration.

See *The PLC+ Playbook* pages referenced in the chart that follows, "Five Commonalities of Cohesive Teams."

NOTES

_____

_____

_____

_____

_____

_____

_____

_____

_____

_____

_____

TABLE 3.3

FIVE COMMONALITIES OF COHESIVE TEAMS

Commonality	Location in *The PLC+ Playbook* **Are there other modules that you believe correlate with this commonality of a cohesive team? If so, add them to your work**	Plan for Implementing
Agreed Upon Set of Core Values	Module 2, pages 11–14 Are there other modules that you believe correlate with this commonality of a cohesive team? If so, add them to your work	
Leverage Toward a Noble Cause	Module 1, pages 1–10 Are there other modules that you believe correlate with this commonality of a cohesive team? If so, add them to your work	
Clear Outcomes of Significant Impact	Module 1, pages 1–10 Are there other modules that you believe correlate with this commonality of a cohesive team? If so, add them to your work	
Recognize and Acknowledge Assets	Module 2, pages 14–16 Are there other modules that you believe correlate with this commonality of a cohesive team? If so, add them to your work	
Plan for "What to Do"	Module 2, pages 14–16 Are there other modules that you believe correlate with this commonality of a cohesive team? If so, add them to your work	

ESTABLISHING PLC+ ROLES

The result of your work in the previous reflections and catalyst tasks prepares you and your colleagues for the natural establishment of roles. Much like participants in the instructional leadership team of SCPS, once members of the PLC+ have zeroed in on the four crosscutting values, gained a deep understanding of the PLC+ framework, see the outcomes as significant for teaching and learning, and recognize and acknowledge the strengths they bring to the PLC+, they are likely to take action by stepping into roles that align with those strengths.

In any effective collaborative structure, there is a need for division of labor. Levi (2014) notes that roles are one of the "basic building blocks" of a team's success, describes the roles and responsibilities in an effective group, and explains how each role relates to what others in the group are doing (p. 69).

Individual ownership of specific duties engages team members by allowing them to work in their areas of strength, and working for the good of the whole creates positive interdependence. Members can be assigned multiple roles within the PLC+ framework.

The following is a brief description of a set of aligned qualities for the important roles PLC+ team members can assume.

TABLE 3.4

IMPORTANT ROLES IN YOUR PLC+ AND KEY QUALITIES FOR SUCCESS

ROLE	DESCRIPTION	QUALITIES RECOMMENDED
Team Activator	• Keeps team focused on the foundational pieces of the PLC+ process and consistently moves the learning of the group forward	• Strong collaborator • Trusted and respected by team members • Has knowledge of effective, research-based instructional practices
Engaged Participant(s)	This role applies to *everyone* on the team. Meeting success is based much more on the informed participation and input of PLC+ team members than on one person in authority, an expert, or an appointed leader (Garmston, 2012, p. 28). • Comes prepared and on time to meetings • Knows his or her strengths and weaknesses as a contributor and *activator*	• Able to focus attention on the immediate agenda, topics, challenges, and opportunities and eliminate unnecessary distractions for the time being

(Continued)

TABLE 3.4 (Continued)

ROLE	DESCRIPTION	QUALITIES RECOMMENDED
	• Stays focused on the meeting's specific tasks and on the PLC+'s overarching purposes • Listens and responds carefully to others • Contributes respectfully and with the motive of moving the team forward	
Note-Taker	• Keeps a record of the important information generated by the PLC+ meetings • Coordinates communication of minutes to all stakeholders within agreed upon and realistic time frame • Sends agenda and any pertinent information to stakeholders to read or understand prior to the meeting	• Organized summarizer • Meets deadlines • Effective writer and communicator
Data Technician	• Activates the charting of data and other evidence • Compiles data from members of PLC+ team into a usable format prior to meetings • Creates and develops charts, graphs, spreadsheets, and other representations of data and evidence	• Organized • Enjoys working with data • Effective at Excel or other data software • Able to condense student evidence and data into usable charts and graphs
Instructional Researcher	• Researches effective research-based instructional strategies • Provides deeper insights into how strategies can be used and implemented as possible solutions to address students' identified needs related to guiding question #2 of the PLC+ framework	• Can be multiple individuals within the PLC+ • Knowledgeable of educational research and effective instructional practice • Desires to seek out new strategies to support both adult and student learning needs
Timekeeper	• Helps PLC+ team stay on track with time frames agreed upon for agenda items, guiding questions, and discussion or decision points • Makes sure to utilize an external timer and to set it with an audible alarm to keep agenda moving and ensure team focus does not get unnecessarily off track	• Willingness to keep team focused on time commitments • Able to decide when to interject—e.g., when time commitments must be adhered to in order to allow the team to stay on track with time constraints—and when to allow more time than initially planned

ROLE	DESCRIPTION	QUALITIES RECOMMENDED
	• However, recognizes when to let the time expire and not stop the productive dialogue that may be occurring at that moment	
Data Wall Curator	• These members maintain team data displays to communicate the effectiveness of strategies being implemented aligned with evidence of the impact of these strategies in helping to accelerate student learning • Can coalesce data and evidence into usable charts and graphs for both the PLC+ team and other school stakeholders	• Creative in nature • Willing to devote time to developing displays of student data and evidence for both internal PLC+ use and public (schoolwide) use

 Visit resources.corwin.com/plcactivator for a downloadable version of this table.

Be the Catalyst: Previously, we explored the idea of local contexts and the need for adaptations. Using a highlighter, marker, and/or sticky notes, edit or adapt the above roles to reflect your local context. Better yet, share this information with your PLC+, and, as a group, adapt the roles to meet the local strengths of your PLC+. Change what you and your colleagues believe is necessary to make these roles work in your local context.

STEPPING INTO ROLES MATCHED TO PLC+ TEAM MEMBER STRENGTHS

While many of the tasks are ones every member of the team can perform, some will be more suited to particular individuals. Team members often gravitate toward roles that are in their "wheelhouse." But *activators* should not simply assign colleagues to roles based on what *activators* perceive their colleagues' strengths to be. After all, we have devoted a significant amount of time in this part and in previous parts to working on collaboration. PLC+ teams should also work together collaboratively to choose roles that fit each member's strengths. Let's take a closer look at the description of each role and of the qualities needed for effectiveness in each role.

Note-Taker: This role should be assumed by a member of the team who is able to use the most appropriate available technology to record information accurately for the PLC+—e.g., how the team is using the guiding questions or the modules in the playbook—while still remaining an active participant of the meeting. This person must also understand timelines and be able to deliver agendas and minutes of the meetings in a timely manner to all stakeholders.

- Who can multitask well during the meetings?

- Who can capture ideas, strategies, and information in a manner that is usable and understandable and share this material with everyone on the team?

- Who can be relied upon to send out pertinent information to team members consistently before and after PLC+ meetings?

Data Technician: This person is responsible for collecting and compiling data from team members and bringing it assembled to the meeting.

- Who on your PLC+ has the skill and desire to collect and compile data, as well as a passion for organizing information into useful charts that the PLC+ can utilize?

- Who is good at utilizing Excel™ or other similar software programs?

Instructional Researcher: This person should be a member of the PLC+ who has a deep understanding of evidence-based instructional practices and who is an efficient and goal-oriented researcher. This person must be skilled at distinguishing instructional strategies from student activities.

- Who with the appropriate research skill has a passion and talent for helping increase the instructional toolbox of the team?

- Who will be willing to seek and find evidence-based actions and report back to the team new and innovative ideas and strategies for moving learning forward when the team is addressing guiding question #3?

Timekeeper: This person should be a member of the PLC+ who understands the importance of time, feels comfortable reminding the team of the time, and can participate in the meeting while keeping track of the time frame.

- Who has a knack for helping to keep focus on specific agenda items and for guiding questions in a meeting within its allotted time?

- Who will be willing to interject with colleagues to remind them of agreed upon time frames?

Data Wall Curator: This person should post the data and results in a timely manner. Also, he or she must be able to make visually pleasing and understandable charts, graphs, and other representations of team strategies and student learning evidence.

- Who has the talent to help display team results?

- Who has the desire to create and develop graphic representations of team results and evidence?

Be the Catalyst: Let's again return to the local context and the need for adaptations. Using a highlighter, marker, and/or sticky notes, edit or adapt the above descriptions of roles and characteristics to reflect your local context. At this point in the journey, this should be a collaborative task. In fact, you and your PLC+ colleagues may want to add new roles, eliminate some that we have suggested, and modify the expectations for each role. The main purpose here is to develop roles that leverage the local strengths of your PLC+ and serve as a unique catalyst that renders the processes of your PLC+ framework into action.

ENSURING CLARITY WHEN STEPPING INTO ROLES

Here is a final conversation about the clarity of roles. One of the essential elements of effective activation is providing clarity. Remember the five C's from pages 28 and 29 in this guide? It is important that there is an explicit and clear understanding of what each role entails. Vagueness or ambiguity about the tasks to be completed can cause stress and conflict within your PLC+ (Levi, 2014, p. 69). *Activators* need to ensure that the entire PLC+ team is clear on specifically what each role will entail, as well as on how long each person will serve in a role. Roles can be assumed on an annual basis or can serve as rotating responsibilities. An explicit schedule should be established so valuable time is not wasted talking about team members' responsibilities. We also recommend members experience different roles as opportunities for professional growth (Kayser, 1990).

Dividing Labor Leads to Positive Interdependence: Developing and sharing the labor in tasks provides positive independence. When PLC+ team members establish roles and fulfill them in a way that leads to effectiveness and efficacy, they develop a sense of pride and ownership in the tasks, challenges, and goals they set for each other. They become more aware of their mutual dependence on each other. This is what Harris and Jones (2010, p. 178) called "collective professionalism," in which practitioners work interdependently rather than independently.

TABLE 3.5

ACTIVITY FOR ALL MEMBERS OF THE PLC+: STEPPING INTO ROLES

ROLE	WHO BEST FITS CURRENTLY *MAY BE MORE THAN ONE MEMBER, AND SOME MEMBERS MAY SERVE IN MORE THAN ONE ROLE*	DURATION *FOR THE MEETING, MONTH, SEMESTER, OR YEAR, FOR EXAMPLE*	SPECIFIC TASKS TO PERFORM WITHIN PLC+
Activator			
Note-Taker			
Data Technician			
Instructional Researcher			
Timekeeper			
Data Wall Curator			
Other Roles Needed in OUR PLC+			

 Visit resources.corwin.com/plcactivator **for a downloadable version of this table.**

Be the Catalyst: At the risk of sounding like a broken record, use a highlighter, marker, and/or sticky notes to edit or adapt the roles you outline in the "Stepping Into Roles" chart to ensure these roles reflect your local context. Make edits and adjustments in light of your new learning. **This must be a collaborative task.** Add new roles; eliminate some that we have suggested. The roles must leverage the local strengths of your PLC+ and serve as a catalyst to turn the processes of the PLC+ framework into action.

NOTES

NOTES

Part 4

ACTIVATING YOUR PLC+

Norms and Authentic Instructional Protocols in Your PLC+

Our beliefs about teaching and learning are expressed through the actions of our PLC+. The way we operate within each collaboration exemplifies what we stand for and what we desire in our schools and classrooms. The way your PLC+ team members engage in the work of teaching and learning will ultimately determine the impact you have on both student and adult learning. **Norms** are the behaviors that reflect PLC+ team members' true beliefs. We believe all PLC teams come together with a desire to be as effective as they can in what they are called to do. *Activators* play a critical role in guiding their PLC+ team to establish expectations concerning how all of the adults on the team will act to move learning forward for all. This part of the activator guide digs deeper into that process and offers support to *activators* in doing the following:

- Developing norms that establish the culture of the PLC+

- Making sure these norms lead to authentic work

Remember, if your team doesn't establish roles, it is more likely to miss out on the impact available to those teams that recognize and acknowledge the assets of team members and leverage those strengths to build team cohesion. Before you turn the page and immerse yourself in Part 4 of this guide, we want to introduce two guiding questions for your consideration:

1. What does your PLC+ team believe about its potential to impact the learning of the students it serves?

   _____

   _____

2. How do those beliefs manifest themselves through the work of your PLC+ team?

   _____

   _____

A CLOSE LOOK AT TEAM NORMS

In the previous parts of this guide, we looked in on Spotsylvania County Public Schools as its instructional leadership team engaged in identifying core values, focused on a common cause, identified ways to maximize impact, leveraged members' assets, and mapped out a plan. As you might have guessed, all these activities require the development of and fidelity to norms. Because the SCPS team is composed of highly skilled instructional leaders, differing and, at times, opposing viewpoints will come up in meetings. What sets this instructional leadership team apart from so many others is its members' establishment of and fidelity to norms. Dr. Flenard and her team have norms for operating all meetings. This is evident to any observer or guest in these meetings. Dr. Flenard simply points out, "That is how we do business on this team." Although she makes this statement as if this characteristic of her team is not a big deal, the value in knowing what it means to do business on her team cannot be overstated. Process norms are essential in the success of a PLC+.

Similarly, there are processes for getting the work done in Spotsylvania's instructional leadership team. Much like operating norms clarifying the way of doing business, process norms convey standards regarding member interaction and ensure that all members of her team have clarity around colleagues' viewpoints, perspectives, and beliefs. Dr. Flenard points out that, "Our team works because of our established norms. This ensures that we all have a voice, everyone will contribute, and how we will move forward at the end of the meeting as a unified team."

Let's look at the role of norms in your PLC+.

NORMS ARE THE *HOW* OF THE PLC+ THAT REFLECT OUR *WHY*

We will address three types of norms or protocols that guide teams to engage effectively in the work of the PLC+:

- Operating norms
- Process norms
- Authentic instructional protocols

TABLE 4.1

DIFFERENT COLLABORATIVE NORM PROCESSES

TYPE	DEFINITION	EXAMPLE
Operating Norms	Nonnegotiable norms outlining the *how* for all members of the PLC+. These apply to *everything* we do: scheduled meetings as well as dialogues that likely occur in more informal settings (before and after school, in the teachers' workroom, during debriefing sessions at conferences or faculty meetings, or in impromptu teacher meetings in the hallway).	All PLC+ team members will demonstrate respect for themselves and others at all times.
Process Norms	Behaviors developed for consistent practice by team members as they work through the five PLC+ guiding questions. These behaviors demonstrate the four crosscutting values. Process norms may apply to only *one part* of the PLC+.	During PLC+, we will not assume universal understanding of instructional strategies. We will seek to clarify information for the group.
Authentic Instructional Protocols	PLC+ protocols used at specific times with the specific intention of moving the team's learning forward. These are contained in *The PLC+ Playbook*.	Ensure everyone has a voice. Establish the expectation that everyone will contribute to the conversation the team is having.

ESTABLISHING OPERATING NORMS

The term *norm* is very often ubiquitously used by schools and PLCs alike; their usage conveys a multitude of meanings and expectations concerning adult behaviors in collaborative settings. For example, countless teams describe and post their norms publicly, often as some derivative of the following:

All adults will be *on time, prepared, and respectful.*

The question is this: Are those actual *norms*?

Garmston and Wellman (2016) refer to norms as the skills the adults on the team work on until they become "normal behavior in the group. When this occurs, the behavior becomes normative for new group members, who model their own behavior on the standards tacitly set by group veterans" (p. 42). Being on time, prepared, and respectful should not be things people have to work on to become normal behavior. However, we have all worked with someone, or maybe we are that person, who rightfully earns the nickname

"10-minute late John!" In all seriousness, *activators* aim to guide their PLC+ in developing certain expectations that are simply common expectations, and then they help build team cohesion, so members are always displaying these agreed-upon basics of **how** the PLC+ will carry out the **why.**

Sometimes, there will already be schoolwide operating norms that have been developed for all PLC+ teams. If this is the case, we do recommend that your team utilize these norms, with one caveat. Are these norms rooted in the **why** behind the PLC+? Or do these previously established norms perpetuate compliance, not commitment? Endurance, not engagement? Artificial exercises, not authentic work? Discuss and revise these norms as needed before adopting them as your own.

See *The PLC +*
***Playbook* (Module 4,**
"Setting Norms for
Our Ways of Work,"
pages 35–38).

As *activators*, we are driven to make sure that we leverage our team's cohesion to establish operating norms as a means for providing clarity about the work ahead of us. Saying everyone will be on time, prepared, and respectful leaves a great deal of room for interpretation. For example, instead of the operating norm "All voices will be heard," a stronger, clearer operating norm would be "Every team member is expected to share specific ideas and thoughts at every meeting."

Be the Catalyst: In *The PLC+ Playbook*, find the protocol titled "Setting Norms for Our Ways of Work" on pages 35–38. Using this protocol, plan how you will execute norm setting in your PLC+. Then get to it! There are two things to consider when implementing this protocol.

- Have you and your team completed the analyses mentioned in this specific protocol?
- Are there analyses that need to be revisited or emphasized when setting norms?

Depending on the answers to these two questions, additional background work may be necessary for success. At this point in the *activator* journey, if we have built capacity with our colleagues, this can be a group discussion and decision.

As your PLC+ establishes norms, ensure those norms really do guide the **how** of the work. Consider the vignette for Middle America Middle School in the "Close Look" below. It gives us an inside look at the development of operating norms within this particular PLC+. Do their operating norms align with the definition and example of operating norms outlined in Table 4.1?

A CLOSE LOOK AT DEVELOPING OPERATING NORMS

The seventh grade PLC+ at Middle America Middle School met for the first time three days before the students arrived. Team members were relatively new to each other, as well as new to the PLC+ model. The team had studied the five guiding questions and four crosscutting values of a PLC+, and it had conducted a SWOT analysis. Seth, the team's *activator*, guided the team through the five-step process outlined in *The PLC+ Playbook*, Module 4. Then, all team members wrote down individually on notecards what they felt were the most important team behaviors they would like to see lived out in their PLC+. Next, Seth gathered the cards and read them aloud. The team determined which ones were related to expected behaviors of the team and of each individual member for every meeting. They come up with the following:

Operating Norms for Grade 7 PLC+ Team:

1. All team members will come to meetings prepared and having read or completed agreed upon tasks.

2. The team note-taker will send out the agenda to all team members at least 24 hours prior to the meeting (see operating norm #1).

3. At the start of every meeting, we will take five minutes for an emotional check-in to make sure we are prepared to learn.

SOCIAL AND EMOTIONAL CHECK-INS

As you are activating your PLC+ through establishing your operating norms, it's important to remember the social-emotional needs of your colleagues and yourself. We suggested earlier including some type of check-in operating norm that provides a safe space for all members of your PLC+ to share anything that may be impacting them personally or emotionally. This includes you. While we have spoken of the "businesslike approach" needed and the professionalism called for in all PLC+ meetings, we cannot forget that PLC+ teams are made up of human beings. We must explicitly recognize the demanding nature of teaching—composed of daily ups and downs. Often, teachers will arrive at their PLC+ meeting with the challenges of the profession weighing heavily on their minds. Pretending that these challenges and concerns do not exist or prohibiting them from entering the conversation is equivalent to not incorporating the social-emotional needs of our students in classroom activities and experiences. In both cases, learning will suffer. Having a quick formal or informal routine that allows all PLC+ members in the room to reset themselves emotionally before the meeting begins can pay huge dividends in both focus and building collective efficacy. This is exactly what they did at the Berkshire Junior-Senior High School's PLC meetings, described in the next "Close Look."

A CLOSE LOOK AT DEVELOPING SOCIAL-EMOTIONAL CHECK-INS

Berkshire Junior-Senior High School is an all-boys school in upstate New York. It serves a population of youth that mostly have been removed from their homes or traditional school settings for behavioral reasons or because of court placements or having received significant special education status owing to emotional issues. Since 2010 Berkshire Junior-Senior High School has engaged in implementing the "Seven Commitments of Sanctuary": a commitment to nonviolence, to emotional intelligence, to social learning, to open communication, to democracy, to social responsibility, and to growth and change (Bloom & Farragher, 2013, p. 49). These commitments result in educating strong, resilient, disciplined, tolerant, caring, knowledge-seeking, creative, innovative, cooperative, and nonviolent individuals. Sanctuary is a culture.

Berkshire's PLC operating norm is to have a "community meeting at the start of each meeting to set the tone, identify focus, and help everyone check . . . personal baggage at the door." Bruce Potter notes, "I became superintendent in 2009, and we needed a change in many things: student discipline, safety, achievement, and culture. We knew one of the paths was making sure all of our PLC meetings were focused on improving practice and due to that we needed to make sure we were first building trust, encouraging innovative problem solving, and promoting a healthy utilization of conflict to push each other for best outcomes."

During the community meeting, one person starts off by asking the person sitting next to him or her the following questions:

- How are you feeling today?

  [Do you need a check-in after the meeting?]
- What is your goal for today's meeting?
- Who can help you with that?

Then the person who just answered asks the next person until everyone in the room has a chance to respond. The questions are intentionally designed. How are you *feeling* isn't the same as how are you doing? If members are dealing with a personal issue, such as an ill parent or other personal worries, they are encouraged to share that, to allow their peers to be aware of what may be going on. If that is the case, a follow-up question is asked, "Do you need a check-in after the meeting?" This question conveys a message to the team member: "Hey, we care about you, and are here if you need us."

There is also an opportunity for the team member sharing an issue to gain some awareness. The question allows individuals to process and perhaps become aware of the baggage they are carrying with them and of the need to reset themselves for the next 45 minutes because there is nothing they can do about their personal issues now—and there is a job to do. Focusing a troubled participant's mind on working with peers may be exactly what is needed.

Next, if there are six people in the room and five people have *different* goals for the meeting, that conveys to the *activator* that there may need to be a refocusing period after the community check-in to make sure there are common goals the team is trying to accomplish. Finally, the question "Who can help you with that?" helps the team acknowledge there may be certain members who would benefit from some specific time together, in pairs or subgroups, so the whole group might break up to allow that to happen organically.

Tangible results of this routine included

- Decreased staff turnover

- Decreased use of coercive measures with students

- Decreased critical incidents, staff injuries, and client injuries

- Greater client and staff satisfaction

- More innovative problem solving and a consistent increase in academic achievement

REFLECTION

Return to your work in *The PLC+ Playbook*. Specifically, let's look at the "Setting Norms for Our Ways of Work" on page 37. Look at the list of norms created as a result of that work. Put an "O" by those norms that you would consider operating norms. Put an "SE" by those norms you would consider social-emotional check-ins. If you find that a particular norm cannot be classified as either an "O" or "SE," leave it for now. Discussing these "other" norms is exactly where we are going next.

ESTABLISHING PROCESS NORMS

Once we have developed operating norms, our attention should be directed toward the *process norms*. Process norms are different than operating norms in that they outline the behaviors the PLC+ team desires to see consistently from all team members during collaboration. The PLC+ team has to work at developing process norms as common practice.

Pause for a moment and look back at the previous parts of this guide. Consider your progress through the journey toward becoming an *activator*, and reflect on times and circumstances that have called for process norms. Where do you now see that a process norm is necessary? Create that list here. We will return to this list once we look more at what is meant by a process norm.

Where is a process norm needed?   What might that norm be?

_____

_____

_____

_____

_____

_____

_____

_____

_____

_____

_____

_____

_____

_____

_____

_____

Process norms will be what the team refers to in order to keep the rudder of the team's ship steering in a common direction at a specific part of the PLC+ framework. Similar to learning intentions and success criteria for our classrooms, the process norms necessary for the day's work should be the starting point for that day. For example, when the team works on the first guiding question, the process norm might be this:

When we are addressing "Where we are going?" we will analyze the state standards and curriculum framework (see Table 4.1).

This is the normal and expected *process* norm for initiating the work on guiding question #1. Thus, not all of the process norms are going to be lived out at every part of the PLC+ framework. This is how they differ from operating norms, which provide guidance for **all** aspects of our work.

> **Be the Catalyst:** In Table 4.2, there are several examples of process norms. Just as you previously adapted norms for local contexts, edit and revise these process norms to fit the unique characteristics of your state and district (i.e., local context).

TABLE 4.2

DEVELOPING PROCESS NORMS

PROCESS NORM EXAMPLES	ADAPTATIONS TO REFLECT MY LOCAL CONTEXT
When we address guiding question #1 (Where are we going?): • We will first analyze the district priority standards to know *where we are going*.	
When we are addressing guiding question #2 (Where are we now?): • We will look first for evidence of our committed instructional actions to determine our current impact. • We will consider evidence of these instructional actions a priority when analyzing any student data or products.	
When we are addressing guiding question #3 (How do we move learning forward?): • We will not assume universal understanding of how instructional strategies look in practice. • We will ensure we have a collective understanding when we agree to use specific instructional practices and strategies.	

(Continued)

TABLE 4.2 (Continued)

PROCESS NORM EXAMPLES	ADAPTATIONS TO REFLECT MY LOCAL CONTEXT
When we are addressing guiding question #4 (What did we learn today?): • We will intentionally reflect after every meeting and monitor how our time together moved our team's learning forward.	
When we address guiding question #5 (Who benefited and who did not benefit?): • We will consistently (at least several times per nine weeks) monitor the progress and achievement of all students. • We will not deflect responsibility for the results we are seeing in some learners to reasons that are beyond our control, especially when we engage in conversations related to equity. • We will actively seek different approaches for learners who are not showing growth in their learning. • We will regularly examine assignments and tasks to monitor the level of rigor at which we are engaging our students.	

Let's look in on Seth Greenswold and his PLC+ team as they develop process norms.

A CLOSE LOOK AT DEVELOPING PROCESS NORMS

Once Seth and the team finished their index card activity from Module 4 in *The PLC+ Playbook* and came to consensus on their operating norms, the team then set out to determine what process norms members could agree on. The team had already come up with three operating norms, so participants planned to try to limit their process norms to three or four. Their understanding of the five guiding questions and four crosscutting values of PLC+ was helpful as they developed the following process norms:

A. We will consistently model instructional strategies with each other and seek clarification when needed to understand how to best implement these in our classroom (guiding question #3).

B. We will consistently examine student tasks, homework, and other assignments for rigor and alignment to specific learning needs (guiding question #2).

C. We will consistently monitor all our subpopulations to monitor any equity issues that could arise (guiding question #5).

D. We will consistently use student voice evidence as an indicator (guiding question #4).

E. We will consistently use the curriculum documents developed by the district's vertical teams to develop our learning progressions (guiding question #1).

The team liked the idea of using the word *consistently* in all process norms to remind team members that these actions should happen often. However, where the team was in its inquiry cycle would drive which process norms would be focused upon during a particular meeting.

REFLECTION

Return to your work in *The PLC+ Playbook* on "Setting Norms for Our Ways of Work." Look at the list of norms created as a result of that work (page 37). Put a "P" by those norms that you would consider process norms. You should now have norms that have an "O," an "SE," or a "P" beside them. Take a moment and reflect on the number of process norms, operating norms, and social-emotional check-ins. Does this reflect local context of your PLC+? Does your team need to make any adjustments?

OPERATING NORMS VERSUS PROCESS NORMS

Before moving on to authentic instructional protocols, the **what** of the PLC+, we want to point out one additional aspect of operating norms versus process norms. With regard to timing, operating norms should be in place from the very beginning. Using Module 4 as a foundational task for you and your PLC+ is essential in leveraging the **why** of your PLC+ to carry out effectively and efficiently the **how** and **what**. However, process norms may evolve over time as you and your colleagues develop greater levels of proficiency in your work in the PLC+ (see Figure 4.1). This evolution from basic norms to next-level norms calls for PLC+ to revisit these norms to ensure they reflect the team's current range of experiences, specific expertise, skills, understandings, and knowledge about teaching and learning. After all, the "PL" in PLC+ ensures that we engage in professional learning during our work.

FIGURE 4.1

PYRAMID OF OPERATIONAL AND PROCESS NORMS

Norms have become skills and natural behavior of the team
Collaborative culture is such that the absence of process norms is noticed instantly and addressed seamlessly.

Next level process norms
Inquiry is at the center of meetings; efficacy is pervasive; members are always probing for specificity.

Basic process norms
Pausing and restating of ideas and thoughts are common occurrences; universal understanding is not implied.

Next level of operating norms
Full participation and engagement exist; there are significant contributions from each PLC+ member.

Basic operating norms
Members are on time, prepared, and respectful.

REFLECTION

Let's revisit your work in Module 4, "Setting Norms for Our Ways of Work" one last time (pages 35–37 of *The PLC+ Playbook*). The four crosscutting values should be visible in any norms established in your PLC+. Take a moment and list the four values here:

1. _____

2. _____

3. _____

4. _____

Now, revisit the norms, both operating and process norms, generated in the task in Module 4. As a PLC+, cross-check the team's norms with the four cross-cutting values. Are all the values represented in the norms? Is that representation clear to all members of the PLC+? Which crosscutting values, if any, are not represented in the norms? How could you and your colleagues edit and revise the norms to ensure all of the values are clearly represented in those norms?

See *The PLC + Playbook* (Module 2, page 11).

> **Background Work:** Should you and your team need additional professional learning on the four crosscutting values, take time to review them in the core book and, with your team, complete Module 2 from *The PLC+ Playbook.* You may need to access additional resources beyond the core book and the *Playbook* for additional professional learning.

UTILIZING AUTHENTIC INSTRUCTIONAL PROTOCOLS

As we have said before, authentic instructional protocols are the **what** of PLC+. And, as we have also pointed out, the **what** is driven by the **how** and the **why**. Therefore, the appropriate entry point and applicable tools depend on the **why** you and your team developed in the "Be the Catalyst" task (page 38 in this guide) and the norms (the **how**) that you established in Module 4.

Activators must help the team collectively determine which modules in *The PLC+ Playbook* members will utilize at specific times based on the PLC+ guiding questions. To be clear, we did not imagine that every team engaging in the PLC+ work would complete every activity in *The PLC+ Playbook.* One of the most important PLC+ actions that will lead to greater progress and achievement is utilizing these collaborative structures and protocols at the right time. Teams that utilize protocols within each module of *The PLC+ Playbook* that align with the **why** and **how** of their PLC+ have more reflective dialogue and are more likely to implement highly effective instruction that moves learning forward for both teachers and our students. The modules and each task within those modules are *not* meant to be worksheets that must be completed and submitted to the instructional coach, lead teacher, or building-level administrator. Reflect on all of the work we have engaged in over the past several sections of this guide: collaborative maturity, team cohesion, adaptations to local contexts, clarity about the why of PLC+, establishing norms, and leveraging the wide range of experiences, specific expertise, skills, understandings, and knowledge about teaching and learning. Then, collaboratively with your team, find the appropriate entry point and applicable tools that will work most effectively with your team.

Be the Catalyst: *The PLC+ Playbook* is full of protocols that are aligned to the guiding questions and crosscutting values. Some of them are time intensive. As the *activator,* you will need to seek thoughts and ideas from the team regarding which ones best serve your PLC+ and at what times. Using a cooperative learning strategy of your choice, plan a professional learning experience for you and your colleagues. The purpose of this professional learning experience is to familiarize you and your colleagues with the modules associated with the five guiding questions. The deliverable for this professional learning experience is to find collectively the appropriate entry point and the applicable tools that your PLC+ finds most helpful in your work. Don't forget the work we have done on team cohesion and establishing roles that leverage strengths within your PLC+. Yes, this is a synthesis task. Use the additional space below to map out this professional learning experience.

_____

_____

_____

_____

_____

_____

_____

_____

_____

_____

_____

_____

_____

_____

_____

_____

_____

_____

_____

_____

_____

_____

_____

_____

Part 5

ACTIVATING THE FIVE ESSENTIAL QUESTIONS AND FOUR CROSSCUTTING VALUES OF YOUR PLC+

The next part of this guide assimilates all the work we have done over the past several parts to implement the PLC+ framework and develop other *activators*. A high-impact PLC+ happens in our schools and in classrooms every day when we make intentional, purposeful decisions about teaching and learning. What we do in our PLC+ meetings drives knowledge about teaching and learning in our school and deeply impacts whether both teachers and students learn on deep levels. It's critical for PLC+ members to use the guiding questions to focus their discussions, dialogue, and inquiry process. These questions were designed to move the learning of the team forward consistently by making the PLC+ about the teacher.

The guiding questions should not become buzzwords, wallpaper, or a worksheet to be completed and submitted to the instructional coach. Each one is rooted in research on what works best and should be viewed and understood as a necessary element of the framework. The questions weave together in meaningful ways but can also stand alone as a driver of discussions about teaching and learning. Likewise, the crosscutting values of activation, equity, expectations, and self and collective efficacy are nonnegotiable to the work of the PLC+. Each of those crosscutting values is interwoven into the PLC+ framework and *also* drives the discussion, dialogue, and inquiry about teaching and learning.

So, let's get to it!

iStock.com/RuslanDashinsky

A CLOSE LOOK AT ACTIVATING THE FIVE ESSENTIAL QUESTIONS AND FOUR CROSSCUTTING VALUES

Spotsylvania County Public Schools is just starting a journey to reinvigorate its PLCs. The decision of the instructional leadership team to engage in PLC+ led members to look at their own why, how, and what. Dr. Flenard's unwavering focus on student learning through the implementation of what works best required that teachers focus on what works best in their own students' learning. As you may recall, they identified from the very beginning that the *successful* implementation of PLC+ in a district with 29 different locations required careful identification of and persistent support for the initial *activators*, as these educators would serve as the catalyst for rendering action and accelerating this revitalization of SCPS's PLCs. Without the initial *activators* embracing this particular crosscutting value, the PLC+ initiative would likely spiral into "another meeting."

SCPS also recognized the need to provide the necessary professional learning for the *activators*. This is a matter of ensuring credibility with our colleagues as we engage in compelling but often difficult conversations in our PLC+.

Dr. Flenard and her instructional leadership team acknowledged that the credibility of the *activator* required that he or she

1. Demonstrate competence by having a strong understanding of the PLC+ framework and the four crosscutting values. This includes knowledge of the research behind each aspect of the PLC+ and fluency with the tools in *The PLC+ Playbook*.

2. Embody trust: the *activator* must exercise complete discretion in what is shared outside of the PLC+ and respect the confidentiality of conversations between colleagues.

3. Be immediate with colleagues in the PLC+. This means that the *activator* must be accessible and relatable in every aspect of this work.

4. Exude dynamism in engaging with the five guiding questions and focusing on the crosscutting values. An *activator* must be able to communicate her or his enthusiasm for teaching and learning.

Dr. Flenard and her team will move forward in their work by ensuring that the initial *activators* have multiple opportunities to review the guiding questions, develop their knowledge of the research, and make meaning around why each question is a necessary part of the PLC+ framework. Further, she and her instructional leadership team will provide professional learning related to the challenges that may come from this work. Together, they will develop suggestions for overcoming those challenges with their colleagues, for building a repository of questions and sentence starters to guide their PLC+ teams through these challenges, and for utilizing *The PLC+ Playbook* for support. That is exactly what we are doing in this part of the guidebook.

See *The PLC+ Playbook* (Module 3, page 22) and *PLC+: Better Decisions and Greater Impact By Design* (pages 15–17).

REFLECTION

Please find the section on teacher credibility located on pages 15–17 in Chapter 1 of the core book. Also, look at page 22 in Module 3 of *The PLC+ Playbook*. This task asks you to "talk about each characteristic of teacher credibility" listed in the book. Retrieve the definitions of the four characteristics of teacher credibility. Make sure that you are able to teach these characteristics to someone else in your school. In the space below, list the ways you can strengthen your credibility with your colleagues. Keep this list close by as we move through the next parts of this guide.

_____

_____

_____

_____

_____

_____

_____

_____

_____

_____

_____

_____

_____

_____

_____

_____

_____

_____

_____

_____

_____

ACTIVATING GUIDING QUESTION 1: WHERE ARE WE GOING?

PLC+ Framework Guiding Questions

1. **Where are we going?**

2. **Where are we now?**

3. **How do we move learning forward?**

4. **What did we learn today?**

5. **Who benefited and who did not benefit?**

The question "Where are we going?" is the launching point for every PLC+. This question focuses attention on the intentions for learning. It challenges us to move beyond pacing guides and curriculum maps to make clear-eyed decisions about the learning path we will blaze.

Keep the end in mind: What is it that we want our learners to know, understand, and be able to do? These goals, of course, are not limited to content learning, and can include processes as well as language development and social and emotional learning outcomes. As PLC+ teams engage in this first question, they will clearly define the learning intentions, success criteria, and learning progressions (or, as our colleagues in Canada say, curriculum expectations) that are rooted in the standards for learning established by their state or province, district, and school.

Background Work: There are several constructs from the research on teaching and learning that are foundational in this first guiding question. *Activators* can enhance their credibility with PLC+ members by building their background knowledge of these constructs. Let's begin. Using the chart below, identify the part of the core book that provides information about the following constructs. Feel free to add constructs you believe were left off of the list. In the third column, list possible resources for building additional background knowledge through your own professional learning.

TABLE 5.1

RESEARCH TIED TIGHTLY TO GUIDING QUESTION 1

RESEARCH CONSTRUCT	PAGES IN *PLC+: BETTER DECISIONS AND GREATER IMPACT BY DESIGN*	ADDITIONAL RESOURCES FOR OUR PROFESSIONAL LEARNING
Teacher Clarity		
Learning Intentions		
Success Criteria		
Learning Progressions		

Now, let's explore the possible challenges that arise when engaging in the first guiding question. These challenges come from our work with districts, schools, and classrooms all over the world. There are common barriers that arise when asking the question "Where are we going?" However, when we look past the way a challenge or barrier presents itself and try to understand the reasons for its appearance, the path to addressing or overcoming the challenge or barrier becomes clear. Take a look at Table 5.2.

TABLE 5.2

RESPONDING TO CHALLENGES WHEN ACTIVATING QUESTION 1: WHERE ARE WE GOING?

POTENTIAL CHALLENGES WHEN ACTIVATING QUESTION 1: WHERE ARE WE GOING?	POSSIBLE REASONS FOR THIS CHALLENGE	WAYS TO ADDRESS / OVERCOME	SENTENCE STARTERS AND QUESTIONS
Your PLC+ does not agree on which standards to analyze.	Your district or school does not have a curriculum framework, pacing guide, or blueprint that identifies the priority standards. PLC+ team members have their "favorite" topics or lessons and try to align these to academic standards with that topic or lesson. PLC+ team members feel challenged having to teach and assess certain standards, leading to avoidance of some standards.	Process norms and tools from *The PLC+ Playbook* will be critical in guiding the group away from conversations that do not answer the question "Where are we going?" Ensure that the district or school curriculum documents are readily available to your PLC+.	• *Have we examined the current district list of priority standards?* • *Are we hung up on which standards are really our priorities and which ones are supporting?*
Your PLC+ identifies too many standards to analyze.	You and your team may be trying to "teach everything" rather than focusing on the essential skills, knowledge, and understandings. Your district or school's pacing guides are too complex, listing far too many standards and leaving PLC+ team members with a perceived expectation to teach them all in a small amount of time.	One of the key ways that *activators* can lead the team in the right direction is ensuring the team takes time to analyze specific standards being considered for an upcoming unit of study or inquiry cycle. Listing out all the concepts and skills on one sheet or screen can help teams see when there is too much for the team to ensure students learn everything.	• *Let's analyze all three of these standards one at a time. I will project them on the screen, and we can do these together to identify what concepts and skills are common in all of them.*

POTENTIAL CHALLENGES WHEN ACTIVATING QUESTION 1: WHERE ARE WE GOING?	POSSIBLE REASONS FOR THIS CHALLENGE	WAYS TO ADDRESS / OVERCOME	SENTENCE STARTERS AND QUESTIONS
Your PLC+ team is struggling with the development of learning intentions, success criteria, and learning progressions.	This could be the case for many teams as ensuring "teacher clarity," including learning progressions, learning intentions, and success criteria, is a different way of looking at teaching and learning. For example, the current approach to clarity may be the traditional method of writing standards or "The student will be able to . . ." system.	Develop a professional learning library of resources and examples of learning intentions, success criteria, and learning progressions.	• *We know developing learning intentions, success criteria, and learning progressions is new for all of us. Let's develop some as a PLC+. The more we do it, the better we will get at it!* • *Let's go back to the concept and skills we pulled from analyzing the standard as a starting point. What does the standard say they must know, understand, and be able to do?* • *Is there any essential vocabulary in the standards we need to ensure students understand?* • *Are there any skills and concepts not captured in this standard that could impede a student's ability to access it?*

NOTES

_____

_____

_____

_____

_____

_____

_____

You and your colleagues know your PLC+ better than we do. Take a moment and revisit Table 5.2. Using the highlighter, marker, and tabs that you have relied on during our journey together, edit and revise the content in Table 5.2. What barriers did we leave out? What other ways would you address or overcome the barriers and challenges for this question? Do you have other sentence starters or questions to add?

_____

_____

_____

_____

_____

_____

_____

_____

Be the Catalyst: Modules 5 and 6 in *The PLC+ Playbook* contain the tools for navigating this first guiding question. Spend time gaining familiarity with these tools. Begin to identify the tools that you and your PLC+ will utilize in addressing where are we going. These tools should address the challenges or barriers in Table 5.2. List those tools here and any notes you want to include about how you will *activate* the tools.

_____

_____

_____

_____

_____

_____

_____

_____

_____

_____

_____

ACTIVATING GUIDING QUESTION 2: WHERE ARE WE NOW?

PLC+ Framework Guiding Questions

1. **Where are we going?**
2. **Where are we now?**
3. **How do we move learning forward?**
4. **What did we learn today?**
5. **Who benefited and who did not benefit?**

Having established learning intentions, success criteria, and learning progressions, PLC+ teams can begin to engage in initial assessment of student learning through work samples, student interviews, and pre-assessments. After all, there is no point in teaching something that students already know. There is considerable evidence that valuable classroom time is spent on content that students have already mastered (e.g., Engel, Claessens, & Finch, 2013). However, this particular question can reveal biases about student learning and particular groups of students. The effective navigation of this question requires us to be aware of those biases and recognize them when they infiltrate the PLC+ collaborative team meeting.

Background Work: There are several constructs from the research on teaching and learning that may inform our response to this second guiding question. *Activators* can enhance their credibility with PLC+ members by building their background knowledge of these constructs. Let's begin. Using the chart below, identify the part of the core book that provides information about the items listed in the first column. Feel free to add what you believe we left off our list. In the third column, list possible resources for building additional background knowledge through your own professional learning.

TABLE 5.3

RESEARCH TIED TIGHTLY TO GUIDING QUESTION 2

RESEARCH CONSTRUCT	PAGES IN *PLC+: BETTER DECISIONS AND GREATER IMPACT BY DESIGN*	ADDITIONAL RESOURCES FOR OUR PROFESSIONAL LEARNING
Deficit Thinking		
Pre-assessment		
Data Teams		
Biases		
Problems of Practice		

Now, let's explore the possible challenges that arise when engaging in this second guiding question. There are common barriers that arise when asking the question "Where are we now?" Just as in the first guiding question, when we look past the way a challenge or barrier presents itself in our PLC+ and try to understand the reasons behind the challenge, the path to addressing or overcoming the barrier becomes clear. Take a look at Table 5.4.

TABLE 5.4

RESPONDING TO CHALLENGES WHEN ACTIVATING QUESTION 2: WHERE ARE WE NOW?

POTENTIAL CHALLENGES WHEN ACTIVATING QUESTION 2: WHERE ARE WE NOW?	POSSIBLE REASONS FOR THIS CHALLENGE	WAYS TO ADDRESS / OVERCOME	SENTENCE STARTERS AND QUESTIONS
Your PLC+ is examining end-of-chapter or end-of-unit assessments to determine current student learning needs; i.e., assessment data are rudimentary and generally occur only after teaching.	This can occur when our PLC+ has limited assessment tools at its disposal. It can also happen when we view students' learning in a somewhat linear manner specific to textbook or other curricular documents.	Introducing evidence from *initial* assessments is a great way to get the team looking at evidence of student learning early in units of instruction or inquiry cycles. Doing so will help the team focus discussions on learning progressions and how to intervene earlier as well as be more purposeful in determining how to move learning forward.	• *We've been focusing on post-assessment evidence as our primary method to determine where our students are at the end of a teaching cycle. How could we find out much earlier where they are?* • *Let's examine where our students are related to the learning progressions.*
Your PLC+ team does not engage in the analysis of student work samples.	This will likely happen if examining student work is not a norm in a PLC+. Also, this can happen if there is a culture of grading or the practice of scoring or grading student work during PLC meetings.	As the *activator*, providing an opportunity for scoring and analyzing pieces of student work is the starting point. In the beginning, it is important that these work samples are addressing the same content. Model the process so that colleagues can address their apprehension about the process.	• *Before we go to examine our student work, let's review why we used this assignment / these tasks to determine where students are in their learning.* • *What sticks out to you in the students' responses? What does it tell us about where they are in relation to the learning progressions? What does it not tell us?*

(Continued)

TABLE 5.4 (Continued)

POTENTIAL CHALLENGES WHEN ACTIVATING QUESTION 2: WHERE ARE WE NOW?	POSSIBLE REASONS FOR THIS CHALLENGE	WAYS TO ADDRESS / OVERCOME	SENTENCE STARTERS AND QUESTIONS
Your PLC+ does not utilize common assessments—everyone uses a different assessment.	This occurs in a PLC+ when individual members sit as a group but, once they return to their classrooms, work in "silos."	This is a challenge for many PLC+ teams. If this is the case, before an examination of data or assessment evidence that is not exactly alike, the team needs to devote time to determine what pieces of each assessment have some commonalities. For example, teachers of different subjects could examine student work that contains common learning across content areas: • **Science:** teachers could examine work samples specifically for students' ability to isolate variables, to follow the steps of the scientific method, or to defend a hypothesis. • **Social Studies:** teachers could look for how students were able to use textual evidence to demonstrate cause and effect (e.g., in relation to wars or political beliefs). • **ELA:** teachers can look at written responses to prompts to assess how students were able to draw inferences from textual evidence that was both explicit and implicit.	• *As we examine the assessment evidence today, let's review what common concepts and skills each one of our assessments addressed in common.* • *What do we see in the student work in your subject that applies to other subjects?*

POTENTIAL CHALLENGES WHEN ACTIVATING QUESTION 2: WHERE ARE WE NOW?	POSSIBLE REASONS FOR THIS CHALLENGE	WAYS TO ADDRESS / OVERCOME	SENTENCE STARTERS AND QUESTIONS
Your PLC+ team members each interpret data differently in their analyses.	This likely occurs when each member of our PLC+ is viewing the student data / evidence with a different lens or from a different perspective. In some cases, this may be the result of biases in our thinking about teaching and learning.	All *activators* will have to address this common situation at some point. When this happens, we must remember not to let it derail the discussion. We must help the PLC+ members understand that when this happens, we are seeing things differently, not wrongly. The way the discussion is framed will be very important to keep the focus on what needs in student learning can be identified and not on who is at fault.	*We seem to be making different inferences from the data.* • *Why do we think that is the case?* • *What can we see / hear from each other that makes sense?* • *Is it possible we / you are both right?* • *Is it possible we / you are both missing something?*
Your PLC+ members are deflecting critical discussions and blaming each other as to why assessments of student learning look the way they do.	There could be many reasons for this: • Teachers may feel the students came in significantly behind and the teaching-assessment time frame was shorter than "needed." • Teachers may feel the assessment itself was not fair to the students based on the abilities and/or gaps they brought to the table with them. • Perhaps there is an identity trigger so that the results are perceived as a direct reflection on the PLC+ and the efforts and abilities of its members as teachers.	*Activators* must know how to let individuals vent and share their frustrations without allowing the team to move into lamenting or making excuses. We must focus on how to respond to the data by using learning progressions that were identified during question #1: *Where are we going?* This will lead us to the third guiding question.	• *Can we collectively make a commitment to looking at the data with a solution-oriented lens?* • *Can we examine some of the learning progressions we have been focusing on, the ones we noticed after the initial assessment?* • *What do we see in the data that we are empowered to influence and impact?* • *Does anyone have knowledge of effective strategies to use to support us as we address some of the external challenges we are having?*

(Continued)

TABLE 5.4 (Continued)

POTENTIAL CHALLENGES WHEN ACTIVATING QUESTION 2: WHERE ARE WE NOW?	POSSIBLE REASONS FOR THIS CHALLENGE	WAYS TO ADDRESS / OVERCOME	SENTENCE STARTERS AND QUESTIONS
			• *Yes, we are facing some challenges with some of our students, but we have to examine the evidence for what it tells us about how to move forward.* • *What I wish we would focus on more right now is what the data are actually telling us. What can we learn from this evidence?* • *Some of the arguments we are making about these results are valid. However, we have to focus on what we can control, which is moving the students' learning forward.*
Student voices are not a part of the PLC+ initial assessments.	For some of our colleagues, students' evaluations of their own learning are not viewed as critical in understanding where we are now.	As the *activator*, develop ways to incorporate student voices into initial assessments.	• *We need to get a full picture of where students are in their learning. We have a great deal of student data, but we need to bring in some specific student-voice evidence as well. What do we think of the examples in Module 7?* • *All of us agree we need to bring more student voices to the table. What do we want to know? What questions do we feel we need to ask them?*

Take a moment and revisit Table 5.4. Using the highlighter, marker, and tabs that you have relied on during our journey together, edit and revise the content in Table 5.4. What barriers did we leave out? What other ways would you address or overcome the barriers and challenges that this question occasions? Do you have other sentence starters or questions to add?

Be the Catalyst: Modules 7, 8, and 9 contain the tools for navigating this second guiding question. Spend time gaining familiarity with these tools. Begin to identify the tools that you and your PLC+ will utilize in addressing where its members and the educators and students it serves are now. These tools should address the challenges or barriers in Table 5.4. List those tools here and any notes you want to include about how you will *activate* the tools.

_____

_____

_____

_____

_____

_____

_____

_____

_____

ACTIVATING GUIDING QUESTION 3: HOW DO WE MOVE LEARNING FORWARD?

PLC+ Framework Guiding Questions

1. **Where are we going?**

2. **Where are we now?**

3. **How do we move learning forward?**

4. **What did we learn today?**

5. **Who benefited and who did not benefit?**

Now that we know where we are headed, we can tackle the question "How do we get there?" At this point, it's time to ask guiding question #3: "How do we move learning forward?" This can be a challenge. You and your PLC+ are bombarded with tricks, ideas, and strategies from many different sources. At times, decisions about "what to do on any given day" leave us either trying anything or relying on a favorite strategy, without evidence of its impact. This question requires you and your PLC+ colleagues to assimilate the answers to the first two questions into a purposeful and intentional decision about what works best to move learning forward. This forward movement could require all team members to engage in furthering their own professional learning, or it might mean changing their approach to teaching one particular skill or content area.

Background Work: Again, to enhance our credibility with the PLC+, let's build our background knowledge of constructs associated with moving learning forward. Notice that some of these constructs are directly related to student learning, and some are related to our own learning. Using the chart below, identify the part of the core book that provides information about the listed constructs. Feel free to add constructs you believe we left off our list. In the third column, list possible resources for building additional background knowledge through your own professional learning.

TABLE 5.5

RESEARCH TIED TIGHTLY TO GUIDING QUESTION 3

RESEARCH CONSTRUCT	PAGES IN *PLC+: BETTER DECISIONS AND GREATER IMPACT BY DESIGN*	ADDITIONAL RESOURCES FOR OUR PROFESSIONAL LEARNING
Evidence-Based Practices		
Compensatory and Adaptive Approaches		
Learning Walks / Instructional Rounds		
Microteaching		

As we have done with the two previous questions, let's explore the challenges and barriers that can hinder the work of our PLC+. Take a look at Table 5.6.

TABLE 5.6

RESPONDING TO CHALLENGES WHEN ACTIVATING QUESTION 3: HOW DO WE MOVE LEARNING FORWARD?

POTENTIAL CHALLENGES WHEN ACTIVATING QUESTION 3: HOW DO WE MOVE LEARNING FORWARD?	POSSIBLE REASONS FOR THIS CHALLENGE	WAYS TO ADDRESS / OVERCOME	SENTENCE STARTERS AND QUESTIONS
Members of your PLC+ team could immediately go to their favorite strategies. This might include you!	A favorite strategy might not be related to data, but the comfort level of you and your colleagues could make you gravitate toward it. In addition, we may have limited knowledge of certain effective strategies based on the specific learning needs of our students.	We, as *activators*, must strive to focus on what we know works best versus what we like best to work. What is important is that the conversations focus on how to best pair the learning needs of students with specific strategies and actions.	• *Okay team, let's agree first on what the student learning gap is before we move into strategies. This will help us better ensure they are aligned. My understanding is that we have identified . . .* • *Before we go to what we have done in the past, let's brainstorm some new ideas that are focused on what we see in the students' learning gaps.*
PLC+ team members jump directly to activities rather than instructional strategies.	Activity-driven instruction comes from our focus on what we want our students to do, often overlooking what we want them to learn. In most cases, this jump to activities is unintentional and outside our conscious awareness and that of our colleagues. This just happens!	*Activators* must help PLC+ teams understand what is meant by instructional strategies and how they must align with our learning intentions and success criteria. Instructional strategies are techniques *teachers use* to help students become independent, strategic learners and make progress toward the learning intentions and success criteria.	• *Those are really engaging activities. I like them. Let's do a quick check to make sure they align with our learning intentions and success criteria.* • *I like what you / we are thinking about as possible tasks and experiences for the students; first, though, let's determine how we will guide students in their learning before they engage in the tasks.*

POTENTIAL CHALLENGES WHEN ACTIVATING QUESTION 3: HOW DO WE MOVE LEARNING FORWARD?	POSSIBLE REASONS FOR THIS CHALLENGE	WAYS TO ADDRESS / OVERCOME	SENTENCE STARTERS AND QUESTIONS
PLC+ teams devote a significant amount of time talking about practices and strategies but not about how they will measure the impact.	This can occur when any of the following situations are present: • The PLC+ is using (too) many strategies and trying to throw everything possible toward helping students move their learning forward without stopping to consider monitoring that learning. • The team has been focused heavily on teaching not learning—much more on inputs rather than outputs and impact.	There are several ways *activators* can help guide this discussion so it will have the most impact: • The more focused PLC+ members are on implementing a few solid practices, the better the team will be on executing these with fidelity and quality. • For each strategy determined, develop an agreement regarding how often and to what degree it will be implemented in classrooms. • As each strategy is determined and agreed upon, determine how learning will be monitored.	• *We have come up with some great strategies that are aligned to addressing student learning gaps. We need to make sure we have a plan to monitor whether these strategies are moving learning forward.* • *We have agreed on these strategies. Let's make sure we agree on how often they will be implemented. I was thinking three times per week for 15 minutes. Does that seem like it would be enough?* • *Now that we have agreed upon the following strategies, let's determine what would show us that they are making an impact. What will we look for in student work and performance, as well as behavior?*
PLC+ team members identify high-impact instructional strategies. However, those strategies do not align with the specific learning gaps identified in the data. In other words, great strategy, wrong time.	When looking at evidence-based instructional strategies, we have a tendency simply to treat these strategies as a checklist. If we, as a PLC+, simply "check the box" on using these strategies, we overlook the alignment of those strategies with the specific learning needs of our students.	The role of the *activator* is to guide the discussion toward what the student learning needs are and what the best strategies and actions are to meet those needs.	• *Let's do an alignment check. What are the specific learning gaps we have identified from the data? Let's place the strategies right next to these on the whiteboard. Do we see the alignment we know we will need in order to make sure we are supporting our students?*

Take a moment and revisit Table 5.6. Using the highlighter, marker, and tabs that you have relied on during our journey together, edit and revise the content in Table 5.6. What barriers did we leave out? What other ways would you address or overcome the barriers and challenges that activating this question presents? Do you have other sentence starters or questions to add?

_____

_____

_____

_____

_____

_____

_____

_____

_____

Be the Catalyst: Modules 10, 11, 12, 13, and 14 contain the tools for navigating this third guiding question. Spend time gaining familiarity with these tools. Begin to identify the tools that you and your PLC+ will utilize in addressing how we will move learning forward. These tools should address the challenges or barriers in Table 5.6. List those tools here and any notes you want to include about how you will *activate* the tools.

_____

_____

_____

_____

_____

_____

_____

_____

_____

ACTIVATING GUIDING QUESTION 4: WHAT DID WE LEARN TODAY?

PLC+ Framework Guiding Questions

1. **Where are we going?**
2. **Where are we now?**
3. **How do we move learning forward?**
4. **What did we learn today?**
5. **Who benefited and who did not benefit?**

This question requires PLC+ collaborative teams to look at evidence of learning, reflect on that aggregated and disaggregated evidence of learning, and then move forward with this evidence in mind. This forward movement could require PLC+ team members to engage in furthering their own professional learning, or it might change their approach to teaching a particular skill or content area. Successfully addressing this question will leave the PLC+ laser focused on who did and did not benefit from instruction—the topic of guiding question 5, which we will address at the end of this part of the guide.

Background Work: Using the following chart, identify the part of the core book that provides information about the following constructs. Feel free to add constructs you believe we left off our list. In the third column, list possible resources for building additional background knowledge through your own professional learning.

TABLE 5.7

RESEARCH TIED TIGHTLY TO GUIDING QUESTION 4

RESEARCH CONSTRUCT	PAGES IN *PLC+: BETTER DECISIONS AND GREATER IMPACT BY DESIGN*	ADDITIONAL RESOURCES FOR OUR PROFESSIONAL LEARNING
Reflective Practice		
Expert Noticing		
Common Assessments		

Now let's explore the challenges and barriers that can hinder the work of our PLC+ when asking about what we have learned. Take a look at Table 5.8.

TABLE 5.8

RESPONDING TO CHALLENGES WHEN ACTIVATING QUESTION 4: WHAT DID WE LEARN TODAY?			
POTENTIAL CHALLENGES TO CONSIDER WHEN ACTIVATING QUESTION 4: WHAT DID WE LEARN TODAY?	POSSIBLE REASONS FOR THIS CHALLENGE	WAYS TO ADDRESS / OVERCOME	SENTENCE STARTERS AND QUESTIONS
You and your PLC+ are not clear on which learners are or are not making progress.	The primary reason for this challenge is that we have not devoted time to determining what progress looks like for specific learning outcomes.	Of course, determining progress will come from examining assessment evidence. Determining what to look for before collecting assessment evidence as well during the analysis of student work can support *activators* in moving their PLC+ forward.	• *I have work samples from last year. Let's analyze these alongside our standards to develop a list of look-fors.* • *For this unit, what would we like our learners to be able to do at the end of each day?*
Some PLC+ teams are not used to reflecting on their learning. This often leads to moments of uncomfortable silence or avoidance of reflective practices.	This challenge or barrier appears in our PLC+ for several reasons. In some cases, we do not want to look as if we are not good at our jobs. Another possibility is that our PLC+, school, or district has no culture of reflection.	*Activators* can move their PLC+ out of this type of stagnation by making sure specific routines and protocols are followed for reflection. In addition, team cohesion and the establishment of credibility, efficacy, and collaboration are essential in providing a safe environment for reflection.	• *Okay, those are some good takeaways from what we learned today. Let's try to break some of them down a little more . . .* • *I like what you said there, Karen. We have to go past just acknowledging that there are gaps in student learning and focus on specific levels of the learning progressions. What, specifically, are those gaps? Who else has a thought on that?* • *Tell us again, Sam, what you mean by that . . . ?*

(Continued)

TABLE 5.8 (Continued)

POTENTIAL CHALLENGES TO CONSIDER WHEN ACTIVATING QUESTION 4: WHAT DID WE LEARN TODAY?	POSSIBLE REASONS FOR THIS CHALLENGE	WAYS TO ADDRESS / OVERCOME	SENTENCE STARTERS AND QUESTIONS
You may find that your PLC+ focuses on external factors, factors outside the control of teachers, when responding to what was learned (or not) today.	In this situation, PLC+ team members may feel that the assessment in and of itself was not fair to the students based on each learner's level of readiness. In addition, we may get defensive because we interpret the results as a direct reflection on our identity as an effective teacher.	When this happens, a good *activator* knows how to take a shared comment and transform it into a reflection without it becoming an attack on the person doing the sharing. At the same time, *activators* must make sure the PLC+ focuses on what members have control of in the classroom. Both operating and process norms will help with this situation.	• *The things we are mentioning make sense, but I am going to take us back to our operating norm that says we will focus our efforts and attention on what we can impact. Let's talk about what we have learned here today, about the strategies we are using. . . .* • *The time has come for us to debrief question 4: What did we learn today? Let's go around the table once and each share a reflection. Remember our process norm: "Reflections on question 4 will focus on what we have learned that we can control and impact as a PLC+."* • *Those are all relevant points, but I believe we all agree that our colleagues in the previous grade level are working hard as well. Let's focus back on what we learned about our impact.*

POTENTIAL CHALLENGES TO CONSIDER WHEN ACTIVATING QUESTION 4: WHAT DID WE LEARN TODAY?	POSSIBLE REASONS FOR THIS CHALLENGE	WAYS TO ADDRESS / OVERCOME	SENTENCE STARTERS AND QUESTIONS
PLC+ teams might recognize the learning needs of their students but not the professional learning needs of their own members.	As professionals, we often find admitting our own learning needs to be a difficult act. This difficulty comes from a fear of looking incompetent, being afraid of showing vulnerability, or simply not knowing what we don't know.	This type of reflective practice is important for the *activators* to recognize. There is a tight connection between questions three and four: "How do we move learning forward?" and "What did we learn today?" How is the team examining the impact of the strategies selected to move learning forward? This examination determines what the team is currently learning in its PLC+ journey, as well as what members might *need to learn* as professionals to move student learning forward.	• *Okay, we have been able to agree that, according to the evidence, our students as a whole have some specific learning gaps in. . . . What we have to determine next is what we have to do or learn ourselves to help best support them moving forward?* • *I really liked and appreciated the focus today, team. We have really done a great job diagnosing what the learning gaps are for multiple groups of students, as well as which students need to be pushed forward. What we need to do now is talk about what this means for us as a PLC+ team moving forward. Jim, could you get us started by offering your thoughts?*

Revisit Table 5.8. Using the highlighter, marker, and tabs that you have relied on during our journey together, edit and revise the content in Table 5.8. What barriers did we leave out? What other ways would you address or overcome the barriers and challenges related to this question? Do you have other sentence starters or questions to add?

_____

_____

_____

_____

_____

_____

_____

_____

_____

_____

_____

_____

_____

_____

_____

_____

_____

_____

_____

_____

_____

Be the Catalyst: Modules 15, 16, 17, 18, and 19 contain the tools for navigating the fourth guiding question: What did we learn today? Spend time gaining familiarity with these tools. Begin to identify the tools that you and your PLC+ will utilize in addressing the question of what was learned. These tools should address the challenges or barriers in Table 5.8. List those tools here and any notes you want to include about how you will activate the tools.

ACTIVATING GUIDING QUESTION 5: WHO BENEFITED AND WHO DID NOT BENEFIT?

PLC+ Framework Guiding Questions

1. **Where are we going?**

2. **Where are we now?**

3. **How do we move learning forward?**

4. **What did we learn today?**

5. **Who benefited and who did not benefit?**

This final question in the PLC+ framework takes a critical look at who did and did not make the expected learning gains as a result of our instruction. To answer the question of benefit truthfully and accurately, we must refocus on the learning intentions, success criteria, and learning progressions that provide the definition of benefit. What makes this question so vital to the PLC+ framework is also what makes this question challenging and uncomfortable. PLC+ teams must confront the evidence that points to learners who did not benefit from the instruction delivered by PLC+ members, and they must examine the potential commonalities amongst these learners. One aspect of this question asks whether the learning experiences provided to those underperforming learners are of the same quality as those provided to high-performing learners.

Background Work: Using the following chart, identify the part of the core book that provides information about the following constructs. Feel free to add constructs you believe we left off our list. In the third column, list possible resources for building additional background knowledge through your own professional learning.

TABLE 5.9

RESEARCH TIED TIGHTLY TO GUIDING QUESTION 5

RESEARCH CONSTRUCT	PAGES IN *PLC+: BETTER DECISIONS AND GREATER IMPACT BY DESIGN*	ADDITIONAL RESOURCES FOR OUR PROFESSIONAL LEARNING
Response to Intervention		
Universal Screening		
Tier 1 Instruction		

Now let's explore the challenges and barriers that can hinder the work of our PLC+ when members ask about what we and our students have learned. Take a look at Table 5.10.

TABLE 5.10

RESPONDING TO CHALLENGES WHEN ACTIVATING QUESTION 5: WHO BENEFITED AND WHO DID NOT BENEFIT?

POTENTIAL CHALLENGES WHEN ACTIVATING QUESTION 5: WHO BENEFITED AND WHO DID NOT BENEFIT?	POSSIBLE REASONS FOR THIS CHALLENGE	WAYS TO ADDRESS / OVERCOME	SENTENCE STARTERS AND QUESTIONS
You and your PLC+ find that the instructional strategies you've focused on are addressing only one group (e.g., children in poverty or children with a disability).	This could happen for two very plausible but different reasons: 1. The PLC+ team hasn't engaged in analysis of or dialogue about multiple groups of students. 2. The PLC+ has some issues with, fear of, or resistance to examining the learning and achievement of multiple groups of students.	• One key way to prepare for addressing this issue is to ensure that data are disaggregated by various identifiable characteristics, such as gender, race, SES, mobility, IEP/504, or ELL. • Make this review of the data part of the agenda for any data review meeting—that is, ask, "Do we see any discrepancies in achievement or progress relative to students' demographic or other characteristics?"	1. *How does this strategy impact the various students we serve? (For example, were there differences in achievement and/ or progress related to gender, race, SES, mobility, IEP/504, or other student characteristics?)* 2. *Do we see any discrepancies in achievement or progress relative to student characteristics? If so, what are they?*
Your PLC+ holds learners to low expectations.	There is evidence that teachers hold different expectations for students of different racial, ethnic, and socioeconomic backgrounds. Findings also support the idea that if teachers have high expectations, they tend to have these for all their students. When readiness levels vary, teachers need to find ways to provide pathways for learning for all their students without diluting the rigorous standards to which students need to be held accountable.	Analyzing standards can be a great way to ensure teams are appropriately looking at the rigor level that lies within each standard. As the *activator*, your role is to ensure that your PLC+ has a clear understanding that the level of rigor within the standard is key.	• *Did the tasks that we engaged students in match appropriately the skills and concepts in our standards?* • *Did the tasks that we engaged students in match appropriately the rigor in our standards?* • *Are we scoring student work in alignment with the skills, concepts, and rigor levels in the standards?*

(Continued)

TABLE 5.10 (Continued)

POTENTIAL CHALLENGES WHEN ACTIVATING QUESTION 5: WHO BENEFITED AND WHO DID NOT BENEFIT?	POSSIBLE REASONS FOR THIS CHALLENGE	WAYS TO ADDRESS / OVERCOME	SENTENCE STARTERS AND QUESTIONS
The strategies and tasks shared during PLC+ are surface level and do not induce student learning at deep and transferable levels.	Engaging students in deep levels of learning requires thoughtful planning from the PLC+ members. Ninety percent of activities teachers engage students in are at the surface level, so superficial learning is commonplace in many classrooms. When data show that different subgroups of students are performing differently, efficacy is tested within a PLC+ as teams work to respond proactively rather than blaming others or deflecting blame.	This is an opportunity for the plus in PLC+ to come to life. You can explore and learn about both surface-level and deep learning and about transfer strategies. After this professional development, teams can begin to connect content to instructional tasks and to strategies that include opportunities for surface, deep, and transferable learning. Analyzing standards can also shed light on when deeper learning experiences are applicable and appropriate. In addition, reviewing the indicators on the Hess Cognitive Rigor matrices can help teams explore surface to deep learning tasks.	• *Which standards support opportunities for deep or transfer learning experiences?* • *What surface-level knowledge do students need to be able to engage in deeper learning experiences?* • *What phase or phases of learning are our learning tasks linked to?*

REFLECTION

Revisit Table 5.10. Using the highlighter, marker, and tabs that you have relied on during our journey together, edit and revise the content in Table 5.10. What barriers did we leave out? What other ways would you address or overcome the barriers and challenges posed when a PLC+ activates this question? Do you have other sentence starters or questions to add?

_____

_____

_____

_____

_____

Be the Catalyst: Modules 20, 21, and 22 contain the tools for navigating our dialogue on who did and did not benefit. Begin to identify the tools that you and your PLC+ members will utilize in addressing who did and did not benefit from your teaching. These tools should address the challenges or barriers in Table 5.10. List those tools here and any notes you want to include about how you will activate the tools.

NOTES

NOTES

Part 6

THE NUTS AND BOLTS OF YOUR PLC+

As *activators*, we are initially charged with providing the nuts and bolts of the PLC+ framework. In this chapter, we will provide examples of the structural routines that support your PLC+, such as setting aside time and developing an assessment calendar, and we'll walk you through doing both for your own team. We will also share information about different types of meetings and the typical foci for each. In addition, we will discuss barriers that can arise within PLCs, along with troubleshooting and problem-solving ideas to help you overcome those barriers.

SCHEDULING PLC+ MEETINGS

First, you must determine a schedule for your meetings; this will serve as the road map for your team throughout the school year. There should be flexibility within the PLC+ framework as your meetings progress. **Not every meeting will focus on all of the questions or completely address one of the questions, but every time the PLC+ meets, team members should be acutely aware of what question the team is currently emphasizing, and all members should collaborate to ensure that the team stays focused on addressing that question at that time.**

SETTING ASIDE THE TIME FOR THE WORK OF THE PLC+

As we pointed out at the beginning of this guide, we have not encountered a colleague who is actively searching for ways to fill excess time. In fact, we have experienced the opposite. Our days are full, and time is at a premium. In addition, the variance in school calendars, master schedules, and other meetings in schools makes a one-size-fits-all PLC+ meeting schedule impossible. As you may have noticed, we have never offered a time schedule or meeting schedule for any aspect of the PLC+ framework. Nor have we stated how each meeting should unfold and what specific deliverables should occur at what times. The PLC+ framework is just that, a framework. This framework requires an honest and thorough understanding of the local context and the adaptation of the framework to function within that local context.

As you move into the next "Be the Catalyst" task, consider the amount of planning time you have each day and during the week. The PLC+ framework is designed to adapt to any school calendar and any master schedule. The task that lies ahead for you and your team is making those adaptations for your unique calendar and schedule. There is no right answer here, just the continued focus on teaching and learning within the PLC+ framework.

Be the Catalyst: This task should be done prior to the start of the academic year. Although we recognize that time away from school is needed to energize us for the next year, semester, or quarter, this task is part of the advance planning of your PLC+. Using your school calendar and master schedule, analyze the amount of time available for meetings. Use the template on the following page to begin a list of when you and your team can and cannot meet. For example, if the first Tuesday of each month is set aside for the schoolwide faculty meeting, this meeting time would likely be off limits.

NOTES

_____
_____
_____
_____
_____
_____
_____
_____
_____
_____
_____
_____
_____
_____

PLC+ MEETING TIMES

TIMES THAT ARE OFF LIMITS	POSSIBLE MEETING TIMES

John's daughter and son attend William Perry Elementary School. To support teachers and learners working within the day-to-day schedule, days are identified on the morning announcements. Each morning the principal announces what type of day it is: for example, "Today is an *A Day*." This is not uncommon in elementary schools, and secondary schools use a similar approach. To the outside observer, this announcement of an "*A Day*" is meaningless. To the learners in the classrooms, it tells them about their specials (e.g., art, music, physical education), lunch times, dismissal processes, and activities throughout the day (e.g., club day, library time, hot lunch day). This clustering of processes under designated days helps the learners at William Perry Elementary School know the who, what, when, where, why, and how of their day. Likewise, we can do this with our PLC+ schedule.

A CLOSE LOOK AT PLC+ MEETINGS

Colton Reynolds leads his team through a series of meetings during a unit of study or inquiry cycle. Although they used the five guiding questions with fidelity, Colton and his colleagues changed the titles of the meetings to reflect the local context and shared language in their building. Each year, Colton and his colleagues set aside time before the first day of school to engage in what they call the "getting it going" meeting. This initial meeting sets the tone for the subsequent work, which Colton believes must occur at the beginning of each year and, in some cases, after long holiday breaks.

From that point forward, Colton and his team will base meetings on the specific question that is scheduled to drive the conversation. For example, an "A" meeting is devoted to discussing where the team and the learners it supports are going.

This is only one of many possible paths PLC+ teams can take to stay focused on specific guiding questions during their cycles. Next, let's look at a more general description of Colton and his team's PLC+ meeting cycle. These descriptions, as you might have guessed, were developed during the "getting it going" meeting.

EXAMPLE OF A PLC+ MEETING CYCLE

MEETING DESCRIPTIONS

INITIAL MEETING

Developing a Purposeful Plan. *Every* PLC+ team should engage in an initial meeting at its formation as well as at the start of every school year. If the team has been established as a PLC+ for more than two years, some aspects of these initial meetings, the nuts and bolts of the team's PLC+, would not have to be revisited. However, we recommend that you refresh the team's knowledge and understanding of PLC+ at the start of each school year, especially if new members have been added to the team. In this meeting, the *activator* can lead the team in determining many of the structural and organizational elements required for the team to be successful:

- Determining and/or revisiting the purpose of the PLC+
- Understanding the guiding questions and crosscutting values or refreshing the focus on these
- Setting or revisiting operational and process norms
- Determining when and where meetings will take place
- Assigning roles
- Establishing a calendar for the coming months or longer

MEETING A

Establishing Clarity. At this meeting, members determine what they need students to learn, and the team answers the question "Where are we going?" The focus is on determining specific standards to analyze, developing learning progressions, formulating learning intentions and success criteria, and deciding what initial assessment tools will be utilized in the upcoming unit of study or inquiry cycle, as well as discussing possible post-assessment tools.

MEETING B

Analyzing Where We Are. At this meeting, the PLC+ team examines any initial assessment results to determine where the current level of student learning is for all students served by the team. This would likely be considered a "forest" meeting, meaning the team is looking at student learning as a whole and isn't necessarily looking at individual students (trees). Here is where the PLC+ will determine common challenges as well as any obvious student misconceptions, and it will look into how to best move learning forward.

MEETING C

Moving Learning Forward. At this meeting, the team digs in and determines what adult actions and strategies it agrees upon implementing, as well as how often and to what degree these strategies will be executed. This is also a time for assignment analysis to take place to ensure that what we are asking students to *do* is aligned to what was determined in response to question #1: "Where are we going?"

(Continued)

(Continued)

Monitoring Meeting. This meeting can occur more than once during a unit of study or inquiry cycle. We recommend at least 35–45 minutes for this meeting. Monitoring meetings can be focused specifically on examining the current reality regarding how the PLC+ team's actions and strategies are working.

Determining Impact. This meeting occurs at the culmination of an inquiry cycle or unit of study and at various times within those cycles. At these meetings, team members determine the impact of implemented actions and strategies. The team looks deeply at both progress and achievement and examines evidence to determine if any equity gaps exist.

Important footnote: Our PLC+ teams should not always wait until the end of an inquiry cycle to examine progress and achievement or to look for any equity gaps. Assessing teaching and learning and investigating equity gaps can and should be an ongoing piece of our dialogue and discussion. We recommend scheduling in advance specific meetings for these discussions to ensure they happen with fidelity and regularity.

Be the Catalyst: This "Be the Catalyst" has two parts, which should be tackled in order.

Part 1: Now that we have observed how Colton and his team cluster and identify their meetings, let's look at how their PLC+ allots time for this work. In addition to analyzing the type of meeting, the focus of the meeting, and the desired outcomes, we will leave it to you to visit *The PLC+ Playbook* and list the possible modules that would support your work in each meeting. Fill that information into the fourth column of Table 6.1 only *after* you have talked together about the first three columns. This will give your PLC+ additional collaborative time to consider which modules you think will be helpful to Colton and his team. Once you and your team have finished this task, proceed to Part 2.

Part 2: This meeting cycle may not work for you and your PLC+. Using Table 6.2, a blank version of Table 6.1, collaborate with your PLC+ to develop your own meeting cycle. When creating your meeting cycle, make sure you can come back and make edits and revisions as you engage in your meeting cycle. If Colton and his team's cycle works for you, skip Part 2 of this "Be the Catalyst."

TABLE 6.1

FIVE TYPES OF PLC+ MEETINGS

TYPE OF MEETING	FOCUS / REQUIRED AGENDA TOPICS	DESIRED OUTCOMES / PRODUCTS	*THE PLC+ PLAYBOOK MODULES TO UTILIZE*
Initial Meeting—First PLC+ Meeting 60–90 minutes	• PLC+ framework: Guiding questions and crosscutting values • Determining clear expectations for adult behaviors (norms) • Logistics (e.g., where, when, how frequently for meetings) • Roles and responsibilities • Possible dates for the administration of assessments	• Universal understanding of alignment between PLC+ questions, crosscutting values, adult action, and beliefs about teaching and learning • List of agreed upon expectations for adult behaviors • List of meeting dates and likely topics for next two to three months • Dates / windows for all external as well as internal assessments over the next two to three months or longer if possible • Tentative dates / windows for internal assessments more than three months in the future	
Meeting A—Establishing Clarity 45–60 minutes • Establishing clarity for upcoming unit of study or inquiry cycle **Guiding Questions 1 and 4**	• Determine focus of upcoming PLC+ inquiry cycle • Determine priority or focus standards to analyze • Analyze standards • Determine initial assessment and time for administering	• Analysis of priority standards for unit or cycle • Learning intentions, success criteria, and learning progressions for unit or cycle • Identified or determined initial assessment • Scheduled dates for administering initial assessment • Scheduled date of PLC+ meeting for analyzing evidence from the assessment	

(Continued)

TABLE 6.1 (Continued)

TYPE OF MEETING	FOCUS / REQUIRED AGENDA TOPICS	DESIRED OUTCOMES / PRODUCTS	THE PLC+ PLAYBOOK MODULES TO UTILIZE
Meeting B— **Analyzing Where We Are** 45–60 minutes **Guiding Questions 2 and 4**	• Analyze initial assessment results • Determine common challenges and student misconceptions • Identify gaps related to learning progressions • Determine next steps for answering guiding question #3	• Solid inferences regarding current levels of student learning through analyzing results • Determination of next check-in date • Commitment to bring ideas / strategies for moving learning forward based on common challenge identified • Potential dates for post-assessment administration	
Meeting C— **Moving Learning Forward** 45–75 minutes **Guiding Questions 3 and 4**	• Determine and agree upon strategies and actions for implementation • Assignment analysis	• Instructional strategies that align with evidence gathering • Strategies that move learning forward for all students • Frequency and degree to which those strategies will be implemented • List of tasks and assignments that will be used to best determine if strategies and actions are effective • List of evidence or data to be used in determining the impact of instructional actions and strategies (e.g., student work, assignments, or post-assessments) • An appropriate time for a learning walk	

TYPE OF MEETING	FOCUS / REQUIRED AGENDA TOPICS	DESIRED OUTCOMES / PRODUCTS	THE PLC+ PLAYBOOK MODULES TO UTILIZE

Meeting D—
 Monitoring Meeting
 Length of meeting depends on purpose
 Guiding Questions 2, 3, and 4
	• Determine effectiveness of implemented strategies and actions
	 • Analyze student work
	 • Determine where critical learning gaps exist as well as where challenges still exist
	 • Determine time frame for next assessment
		• Analysis through honest discussion of the strategy implementation and teaching actions as these occurred in team members' classrooms
		 • Collaboratively scored and analyzed student work to determine
		   ○ Success in moving learning forward from strategies
		   ○ Possible student gaps and misconceptions that still exist
		 • Date for post-assessment administration and analysis of results
		 • Schedule for re-teaching essential and foundational concepts and skills, if necessary	

Meeting E—
 Determining Impact
 Length of meeting depends on purpose
 Guiding Questions 3, 4, and 5
	• Determine effectiveness of strategies and actions implemented
	 • Examine post-assessment evidence and data
	 • Determine if any equity gaps exist
	 • Examine progress and celebrate achievement
		• Assessment of the level of impact of actions and strategies on
		   ○ The achievement of all students
		   ○ The progress of all students
		 • Analysis of whether equity gaps are present when any specific learning and/or achievement gaps exist for any specific group of students
		 • Celebration of success when deep levels of learning have taken place!	

online resources   **Visit** resources.corwin.com/plcactivator **for a downloadable version of this table.**

TABLE 6.2

TEMPLATE FOR DEVELOPING SCHEDULE FOR TYPES OF PLC+ MEETINGS

TYPE OF MEETING	FOCUS / REQUIRED AGENDA TOPICS	DESIRED OUTCOMES / PRODUCTS	*THE PLC+ PLAYBOOK MODULES TO UTILIZE*

 Visit resources.corwin.com/plcactivator **for a downloadable version of this table.**

OVERCOMING CHALLENGES: (NOT ENOUGH) TIME

Now let's address a challenge we have previously identified. Although this goes without saying, PLC+ teams that can meet more than once per week will have much more flexibility in predetermining the focus of their PLC+ meetings. They will be much more able to be flexible within the framework when that is needed. This isn't to say they should not develop a schedule with some predetermined dates for specific tasks: e.g., analyzing standards, assessment analysis, or a values check. But teams that have less available time to meet must adapt the framework to work within their limitations. We have had the pleasure of working with schools and districts around the country that have found efficient and effective ways of activating the PLC+ framework and leveraging the four crosscutting values within their tight time frames. What follows are examples that serve as guides for making it work. Specifically, these examples are from teams during their first two years of activating a PLC+. Here are some important points to note:

- In year one, PLC+ teams must commit to following through on several complete cycles (units / inquiry).

- PLC+ teams must devote time to each of the questions and dedicate specific times to digging into the values

- Especially in year one, but also as an ongoing practice, PLC+ teams must allow time for reflection on their own learning—not only to learning related specifically to the PLC+ process and framework but also to the lessons PLC+ is teaching them about their learning and the learning of their students.

TABLE 6.3

EXAMPLE: PLC+ MEETS ONCE PER WEEK YEAR 1

MEETING DATES	FOCUS / GUIDING QUESTIONS	THE PLC+ PLAYBOOK MODULES	ADDITIONAL RECOMMENDATIONS
August 15	Initial Meeting	1, 2	
August 22	Meeting A	5	
August 29	Meeting B	7	
September 5	Meeting C	10, 14	Values check (VC)
September 12	Meeting D	17	Common assessments
September 19	Meeting E	18	

(Continued)

TABLE 6.3 (Continued)

MEETING DATES	FOCUS / GUIDING QUESTIONS	THE PLC+ PLAYBOOK MODULES	ADDITIONAL RECOMMENDATIONS
September 26	"Now What? / So What?"	TBD	Determine some specific things the adults need to learn: • What worked well—why? • What didn't work well—why? • According to the team, what learning needs of the adults on the team need to be addressed?
October 3	Meeting A	5	
October 10	Meeting B	8	
October 17	Meeting C	10 or 11	
October 24	Meeting C	14	Values check
October 31	Meeting D	16	
November 7	Meeting E	20	
November 14	"Now What? / So What?"	TBD	What are some learning pieces the team needs to capture? • What worked well—why? • What didn't work well—why? According to the team, what learning needs of the adults on the team need to be addressed?
November 21	TBD—Status of PLC+ Check-In Meeting		
November 28	No Meeting—Thanksgiving		
December 5	TBD—Based on November 21 Meeting		
December 12	TBD—Based on November 21 Meeting		
December 19	End of Semester 1—Celebration		
January 9	Planning for Semester 2		
January 16	Meeting A	5	

MEETING DATES	FOCUS / GUIDING QUESTIONS	THE PLC+ PLAYBOOK MODULES	ADDITIONAL RECOMMENDATIONS
January 23	Meeting B	7, 8, or 9 (VC)	Commit to a values check in one of these three meetings
January 30	Meeting C	10, 11, 13, or 14 (VC)	Commit to a values check in one of these three meetings
February 6	Meeting D	13 or 16	Commit to a values check in one of these three meetings
February 13	Meeting E	21	Responding to student learning needs—Determine status of response to intervention (RTI)
February 20	Meeting E	22	Values check
February 27	"Now What? / So What?"	TBD	What are some learning pieces the team needs to capture? • What worked well—why? • What didn't work well—why? According to the team, what learning needs of the adults on the team need to be addressed?
March 5	TBD—Status of PLC+ Check-In Meeting		
March 12	TBD—Based on March 5 Meeting		
March 19	TBD—Based on March 5 Meeting		
March 26	NO MEETING— SPRING BREAK		
April 2	TBD—Status of PLC+ Check-In Meeting		
April 9	Meeting A	Team determines	Before school year ends, team follows one more **tight cycle** to serve as basis for planning for following school year
April 16	Meeting B	Team determines	Before school year ends, team follows one more **tight cycle** to serve as basis for planning for following school year
April 23	Meeting C	Team determines	Before school year ends, team follows one more **tight cycle** to serve as basis for planning for following school year

(Continued)

TABLE 6.3 (Continued)

MEETING DATES	FOCUS / GUIDING QUESTIONS	THE PLC+ PLAYBOOK MODULES	ADDITIONAL RECOMMENDATIONS
April 30	Meeting D	Team determines	Before school year ends, team follows one more *tight cycle* to serve as basis for planning for following school year
May 7	Meeting E	Team determines	Before school year ends, team follows one more *tight cycle* to serve as basis for planning for following school year
May 14	TBD	Team determines	Team plans for end of current school year as well as for following school year
May 21	TBD	Team determines	Team plans for end of current school year as well as for following school year
May 28	End of Semester 2— Celebration		

TABLE 6.4

EXAMPLE: PLC+ MEETS ONCE PER WEEK YEAR 2

MEETING DATES	FOCUS / GUIDING QUESTIONS	PLAYBOOK MODULES	ADDITIONAL RECOMMENDATIONS
August 15	Initial Meeting	1, 2	Important to start school year and establish role of PLC+, team focus, and other essentials
August 22	Meeting A	5	
August 29	Meeting B	Team Determines	
September 5	Meeting C	Team Determines	
September 12	Meeting D	Team Determines	
September 19	Meeting E	Team Determines	
September 26	Meeting A	5	
October 3	Meeting B	Team Determines	
October 10	Meeting C	Team Determines	
October 17	Meeting D	Team Determines	
October 24	Meeting E	Team Determines	
October 31	TBD—Status of PLC+ Check-In Meeting		

MEETING DATES	FOCUS / GUIDING QUESTIONS	PLAYBOOK MODULES	ADDITIONAL RECOMMENDATIONS
November 7	Meeting A	5	
November 14	Meeting B	Team Determines	
November 21	Meeting C	Team Determines	
November 28	No Meeting Thanksgiving		
December 5	Meeting D	Team Determines	
December 12	Meeting E	Team Determines	
December 19	End Semester 1—Celebration		
January 9	Planning for Semester 2		
January 16	Meeting A	5	
January 23	Meeting B	Team Determines	
January 30	Meeting C	Team Determines	
February 6	Meeting D	Team Determines	
February 13	Meeting E	Team Determines	
February 20	Meeting A	5	
February 27	Meeting B	Team Determines	
March 5	Meeting C	Team Determines	
March 12	Meeting D	Team Determines	
March 19	Meeting E	Team Determines	
March 26	NO MEETING—SPRING BREAK		
April 2	TBD—Status of PLC+ Check-In Meeting		
April 9	Meeting A	Team Determines	
April 16	Meeting B	Team Determines	
April 23	Meeting C	Team Determines	
April 30	Meeting D	Team Determines	
May 7	Meeting E	Team Determines	
May 14	TBD		
May 21	TBD		
May 28	End Semester 2—Celebration		

 Visit resources.corwin.com/plcactivator **for a downloadable version of this table.**

We recommended that all PLC+ teams, early in their journeys, implement a schedule in year one to develop a plan for several units or inquiry cycles—and that they stay true to these. This allows you and your team to develop a better understanding of what a cycle involves, the complexities of the guiding questions, how to establish a culture for learning through monitoring the operating and process norms, and how to develop and utilize authentic instructional protocols. In addition, moving through several unit/inquiry cycles will build the depth and breadth of the framework necessary for more intentional, purposeful, and deliberate adaptations for future work with your PLC+.

Be the Catalyst: Your turn! With your PLC+ team, build a calendar for your work. Using the above examples, along with your school's calendar and master schedule, discuss and develop the progression of your PLC+ work. There are downloadable, editable versions of tables from this book on the companion website for you to use at resources.corwin.com/plcactivator.

REFLECTION

As you have progressed in your work as an *activator*, how are you feeling? What is working well? What has appeared as a stumbling block? Where can you go to get support to help you avoid stumbling blocks? Use the space provided to create a list of questions or concerns that you and your PLC+ team need addressed, perhaps with the support of a mentor or instructional leader.

_____

_____

_____

_____

_____

_____

_____

_____

_____

_____

_____

_____

QUESTIONS AND/OR CONCERNS	WHO CAN HELP?	HOW THEY HELPED

DEVELOPING AN ASSESSMENT CALENDAR

Before we look at designing an assessment calendar, let's review three types of assessments.

1. **Assessments *of* learning.** You and your team likely have access to assessments that are assessments *of* learning. These assessments are designed to measure the progress and achievement of learners. Examples include

   - Common formative assessments
   - Standardized assessments

2. **Assessments *as* learning.** Assessments *as* learning allow learners to retrieve information that gives insight into how their learning is going, but they also enhance learning simply through the retrieval practice. Examples include

   - Think-pair-share (TPS)
   - Reciprocal teaching

3. **Assessments *for* learning.** Assessments *for* learning allow the teacher to make adjustments to the learning progression based on checks for understanding. Examples of these checks include

   - Exit tickets
   - Three-minute writing

Assessments *as* and *for* learning are readily available for analysis by you and your PLC+. These check-ins help us understand where we are now and what we learned today. Furthermore, they provide a snapshot of who did and did not benefit today. These quick evaluations are also more immediate than other assessments, and this immediacy allows them to be helpful and inform every PLC+ meeting. However, some assessments require more time and measure longer-term progress and achievement, providing a broad picture of learning progression. These are the assessments *of* learning, and they must be scheduled into our PLC+ work.

Developing an assessment calendar will ensure that the team grasps what assessments measuring progress and achievement members will be accountable for administering. The calendar will also serve as a plan for utilizing the evidence from these assessments *of* learning to make solid inferences about student learning.

Activators can set the team up for success by guiding the team into establishing a schedule for any school or district-based assessments. This will involve knowing when these assessments will be administered and when results are expected to be back and available for analysis. From here, the PLC+ can better make use of its internal PLC+ calendar for scheduling any team assessments members will use to answer the questions "Where are we now?" and "What did we learn?" Data from team assessments will provide a clear view of who is and who is not benefiting from our teaching. Building an assessment calendar and spacing out assessments will prevent team overload. When multiple assessments are analyzed by our teams at the same time, we can suffer from the DRIP syndrome (data rich, information poor).

Now let's look at the steps for developing an assessment calendar within the PLC+ calendar you created earlier.

1. Map out when any external or high-stakes assessments will be administered: Smarter Balance™, PARCC, or other state or provincial tests, as well as any relevant national or international assessments (e.g., TIMMS, NAEP, SAT, ACT).

2. Map out any local (district-based) assessments: e.g., district benchmarks, NWEA / MAP, or district common formative assessments.

3. Identify the windows for assessment administration.

4. List the dates (if known) for assessment evidence to be returned to PLC+.

5. Identify PLC+ predetermined assessments: e.g., curricular, unit, or chapter assessments.

Be the Catalyst: As a PLC+, list the external assessments *of* learning administered at your school. Be sure to include **when** they are administered during the academic year and when you and your learners will receive the data generated by these assessments. This might include end-of-course assessments from the previous year.

ASSESSMENTS *OF* LEARNING	DATE OF ASSESSMENT	DATE DATA AVAILABLE

The goal for this next process is to assimilate your state, district, or local assessment calendar into your PLC+ meeting cycle. For example, "What did we learn today?" may need to be moved in the meeting cycle so that this particular meeting occurs after a common formative assessment or other scheduled assessment. Now, look at the example of an assessment calendar in Table 6.5 to see how your list might look in context.

TABLE 6.5

SAMPLE ASSESSMENT CALENDAR

MONTH	WEEK OF	LOCAL BENCHMARK (DATES / WINDOWS)	EXTERNAL / HIGH-STAKES ASSESSMENTS	PLC+ ASSESSMENT TENTATIVE ADMINISTRATION DATES
August	19	Fall MAP Assessments (21–24)		
	26			Semester Initial Assessment* (28–29)
September	2			
	9			Unit 1 Post-assessment (12–13)
	16			
	23			Unit 2 Initial Assessment** (26–27)
	30			
October	7			
	14	District Writing Assessment (15–16) Results Returned to PLC+ Teams 23		
	21			Unit 3 Initial Assessment (29–30)
	28			
November	4			
	11			Unit 3 Post-assessment (12–13)

MONTH	WEEK OF	LOCAL BENCHMARK (DATES / WINDOWS)	EXTERNAL / HIGH-STAKES ASSESSMENTS	PLC+ ASSESSMENT TENTATIVE ADMINISTRATION DATES
	18			
	25			Unit 4 Initial Assessment*** (25–26)
December	2			
	9			
	16			Semester Post-assessment (18–19)
January	6			Semester 2 Initial Assessment**** (7–8)
	13	Winter MAP Assessments (15–17)		
	20			
	27			Unit 5 Post-assessment (28–29)
February	3			
	10			Unit 6 Initial Assessment (10–11)
	17			
	24			Unit 6 Post-assessment (27–28)
March	2			
	9			Unit 7 Initial Assessment (11–12)
	16			
	23			
	30	Spring Break		
April	6			Unit 7 Post-assessment (9–10)
	13		PARCC Window (13–30)	

(Continued)

TABLE 6.5 (Continued)

MONTH	WEEK OF	LOCAL BENCHMARK (DATES / WINDOWS)	EXTERNAL / HIGH-STAKES ASSESSMENTS	PLC+ ASSESSMENT TENTATIVE ADMINISTRATION DATES
	20		PARCC Window (13–30)	
	27		PARCC Window (13–30)	Unit 8 Initial Assessment (28–29)
May	4			
	11			
	18			Semester 2 Post-assessment
	25			

*Unit 1 initial assessment evidence will be gathered from the semester initial assessment.

**Unit 2 post-assessment evidence will be gathered and analyzed by individual teachers due to the timing of the district writing assessment, which will be analyzed by the PLC+ team.

*** Unit 4 post-assessment evidence will be gathered from the semester 1 post-assessment

****Unit 5 initial assessment evidence will be gathered from the semester 2 initial assessment.

 Visit resources.corwin.com/plcactivator **for a downloadable version of this table.**

> **Be the Catalyst:** Using the PLC+ calendar you developed using Tables 6.1 through 6.4, add the schedule for the administration and analysis of these assessments *of* learning. Keep in mind that you and your team may have to edit and revise your original calendar to accommodate these very important analyses.

Before we move into a discussion about high-impact versus high-functioning PLC+, let's revisit our work thus far. Find page 15 in *The PLC+ Playbook*. Even if you have done this before, reevaluate where you and your colleagues are in your PLC+ with regard to the SWOT analysis. Are you and your team able to move opportunities into the strengths category? What about strengths that now, upon further work, yielded opportunities? Like the first time you completed this part of the module, this should be done as a collaborative task—one that encourages open and honest dialogue amongst colleagues. Add your notes in the space below or in your copy of *The PLC+ Playbook*.

NOTES

Part 7

ACTIVATING A HIGH-IMPACT AND HIGH-FUNCTIONING PLC+

An important characteristic of any *activator* is the ability to serve as a catalyst and move your PLC+ team's learning forward; that learning, in turn, amplifies your collective impact on teaching and on student learning. PLC+ teams will have varying degrees of professional learning needs. For some *activators,* serving as a catalyst for professional learning may involve helping to guide your colleagues past indifference and stagnation and toward comfort with learning from and with each other. Other situations may call for *activators* to move their teams from compliance-based meetings, where the group is simply filling out forms and going through the motions of addressing the five guiding questions, to truly engaging in the analysis of teaching and learning. As we make our way to the end of this guide, we want to focus on the challenges and barriers related to the internal dynamics of your PLC+. Put differently, how do we navigate the different personalities in our PLC+?

See *The PLC+ Playbook* (page 5).

NOTES

_____

_____

_____

_____

_____

_____

_____

_____

_____

REFLECTION

Before we move into a discussion about the high-impact versus the high-functioning PLC+, let's revisit the six characteristics of a PLC. Find page 5 in *The PLC+ Playbook*. Even if you have done this before, reevaluate where you and your colleagues are in your PLC+. Unlike the first time, when you completed this part of the module independently, this time it should be done as a collaborative task—one that encourages open and honest dialogue among colleagues. Add your notes in the space below or in your copy of *The PLC+ Playbook*.

HIGH IMPACT VERSUS HIGH FUNCTIONING

In her book, *The Skillful Team Leader*, Elisa MacDonald (2013, p. 5) notes that the most effective team leaders value the following:

1. Collaboration
2. Shared leadership
3. Goal setting and attainment
4. Rigorous discourse
5. Continuous improvement

She goes on to make a clear distinction between teams that are high functioning and those that have high impact on student learning. (See Figure 7.1: The Function–Impact Matrix.) On the vertical axis is the level of functionality of the team or PLC, while the level of impact the team has on student learning is measured on the horizontal axis. *Activators* are the essential link that prevents teams from staying in the bottom left quadrant of the matrix.

FIGURE 7.1

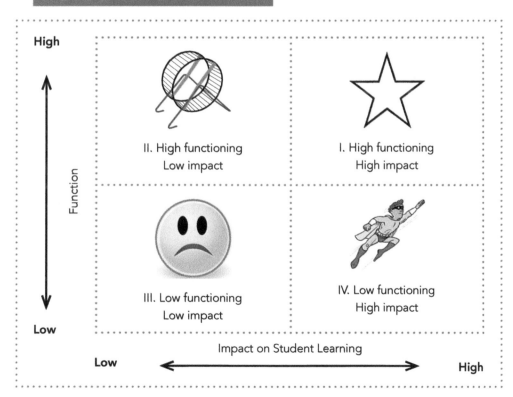

Source: E. MacDonald, *The Skillful Team Leader* (Thousand Oaks, CA: Corwin, 2013), 31.

 Visit resources.corwin.com/plcactivator **for a downloadable version of this table.**

Where is your PLC+? As a collaborative task, determine where you and your colleagues believe your PLC+ fits into the matrix in Figure 7.1. Why do you and your colleagues believe this? How do the five characteristics valued by effective team leaders (MacDonald, 2013) frame your discussion? Do you see these in the dialogue about where your PLC+ fits into this matrix? Use the space below to take notes or capture the essentials of the conversation. Before moving on to the next "Be the Catalyst" task, make sure all members of your PLC+ agree on the notes and that these notes capture the dialogue well.

_____

_____

_____

_____

_____

_____

_____

_____

_____

Be the Catalyst: Revisit your SWOT analysis on pages 15–16 of *The PLC+ Playbook*. If you have completed this task, now would be a good time to check in on your team's progress toward addressing opportunities. If you have not previously used this tool, now would be a good time to complete the SWOT analysis. As the *activator*, develop an engaging and collaborative approach for working with this tool. Use the space below to plan out your approach, whether this is the first SWOT analysis for your team or a reevaluation of the team's previous analysis.

_____

_____

_____

_____

_____

_____

_____

See *The PLC+ Playbook*
(pages 15–16).

Now is the time for you and your colleagues to make any needed adjustments to your PLC+. Combining your work from the two reflections and the "Be the Catalyst" task above, develop some approaches for helping your PLC+ live and thrive in Quadrant I. As you can see in Figure 7.1, MacDonald labels Quadrant I teams as both high functioning and having a great deal of impact on student learning. Table 7.1 provides guidance on how we can lead our teams out of the other three quadrants and move them toward Quadrant I.

TABLE 7.1

PROBLEMS AND SOLUTIONS: MOVING TOWARD QUADRANT I

PROBLEMS AND SOLUTIONS: MOVING TOWARD QUADRANT I	
Quadrant III: Low Functioning and Low Impact This type of PLC+ can often be described as floundering—not functioning well and not having an impact.	This is most challenging task for any *activator* to undertake independently. These PLC teams are easily spotted during any type of observation and can be described as anything from floundering to toxic. *Activators* trying to work with these teams may need to seek support from school leadership. At the same time, it is very important for the *activator* to seek small wins with the team. *Often teams in this quadrant need some very tight structures to be put in place, so members can be guided through the PLC+ process with strong intentionality. Developing and adhering tightly to norms and protocols are critically important.*
Quadrant II: High Functioning and Low Impact These are PLC+ teams that falsely appear to have high impact because they are compared to teams that do are not high functioning. In other words, they look good on the surface!	Obviously, high functioning is important, and quite often this functioning is easy to see and can mask many shortcomings in terms of the team's impact. Many PLC teams that are efficient but don't have a great deal of impact on student learning come together just to complete a series of tasks, follow data protocols, and complete forms. These can be described as compliance-based PLC+ teams. These teams can fly under the radar, as an observer could easily feel there is impact happening. They get along and seem to make instructional decisions that are good for students, but they don't collectively challenge each other to make ones that truly impact students at the highest levels. They, like teams in Quadrant IV, resemble a track-and-field team: team members simply throw in their points or scores (data), but there is little if any positive interdependence. *One of the most important actions for an activator is to make sure there is constant revisiting of question 4, "What did we learn today?" The more the team can focus its efforts on truly looking at what was learned, in an honest and reflective manner, the more the team will be able to examine how it is truly impacting student learning.*

(Continued)

TABLE 7.1 (Continued)

PROBLEMS AND SOLUTIONS: MOVING TOWARD QUADRANT I

Quadrant IV: Low Functioning But High Impact

These are PLC+ that are impacting student learning but are either working excessively hard to do so, or doing so as teachers who work in relative isolation, even on their team. This team could have a much greater impact if they leveraged their individual efficacy into a collective efficacy.

This type of team almost seems like an impossibility. How can a team that is functioning poorly have high impact on student learning? However, this can be the case when team members work in relative isolation.

> A team whose collaboration falls here [in Quadrant IV] is peculiar in that its members function poorly as a group and yet still manage to achieve team goals and advance student learning. They meet together, but they struggle with interdependence. . . . . Any attempt to foster interdependence where team members learn from and rely on one another in a low-functioning, high-impact team often results in conflict, gossip, or withdrawal. Members in low-functioning, high-impact teams who single-handedly take on the goals of the team can feel resentful or can burn out quickly, while others who depend on them can feel helpless. (MacDonald, 2013, p. 31)

While teams in this quadrant may have an overall impact, true collaboration is often nonexistent. What can lead to this? And what can *activators* do to help move such a team toward Quadrant I?

- Poor relational trust and lack of strong professional relationships
- Lack of common standards or curriculum (singletons or heterogeneous groupings)
- Extreme need for member independence; members fear giving up full control of their decision-making process for their classrooms

While activating norms and protocols is important here, nothing can benefit these teams in Quadrant IV as much as focusing on developing common challenges.

online resources 🔎 **Visit resources.corwin.com/plcactivator for a downloadable version of this table.**

REFLECTION

Now, after you have looked carefully at each quadrant and at the ways to serve as a catalyst to move your PLC+ to Quadrant I, consider these questions. Where do you think your PLC+ is now? What are your plans to move the team toward Quadrant I if members are not already there? Use Table 7.2 (Moving Your PLC+ to Quadrant I) to organize your thoughts. If your PLC+ is ready, involve members in this task.

TABLE 7.2

MOVING YOUR PLC+ TO QUADRANT I

MOVING YOUR PLC+ TO QUADRANT I	
What quadrant do you currently see your PLC+ living in?	What actions do you think the PLC+ *activator(s)* should take to move the team toward Quadrant I?

 Visit resources.corwin.com/plcactivator **for a downloadable version of this table.**

> **Be the Catalyst:** Return one more time to your PLC+ calendar developed in Part 6 of this guide. On that calendar, you should have your proposed meeting schedule and assessment calendar. We want you to add one more feature to this schedule. Set aside time for evaluating where your PLC+ is at various points throughout the year. Put an asterisk next to each meeting at which you will do this. Throughout the year, all teams must check in to see if they are still a high-functioning and high-impact PLC+. Yes, that means we may have to come back to this part of the guide and work through new challenges and barriers, ones that were absent in the beginning but have appeared later in our work.

We will close out this part of the guide by addressing some of the challenges or barriers that come when we work with people. We want to provide ideas and strategies for addressing the challenges and barriers related to the relational dynamics of PLC+ teams, and to focus less on the functional dynamics related to the five guiding questions.

1. WHAT IF MEMBERS OF THE PLC+ DO NOT GET ALONG?

One of the barriers that you may experience is the inability of one or more of the collaborative team members to get along. It is likely that each individual faculty member strongly believes in the value of his or her specific content or way of teaching. As a result of these strongly held beliefs, there was a rather lengthy period of time last year when my colleagues simply could not get along. They disagreed on just about everything. So, how do we activate our colleagues when interrelationships are the challenge or barrier? Doing so involves going around, going over, or removing the barrier.

Approach PLC+ Members Individually: To go around the barrier, we may decide to approach each of the members individually to engage in conversation about the intent and purpose of the PLC+ work and how each can contribute to this work. This one-on-one dialogue provides an opportunity for both you and your colleague to gain a clearer perspective on the work.

Refocus the Purpose: To get over the barrier, we can devote a significant amount of time discussing the purpose of the PLC+ framework. During one meeting, an *activator* we know spent time reflecting with her colleagues about what PLC+ was and was not so that the collaborative team could refocus its purpose toward teaching and learning and away from comparisons between colleagues.

Clear the Air: To remove the barrier, you can allow colleagues to clear the air. This approach can be risky, but we should allow the conversation to unfold and simply redirect comments toward teaching and learning and away from personal attacks. Be prepared to involve other supports or mediation, if it comes to that, during efforts to clear the air.

Is this your PLC+? If so, how will you go around, go over, or remove the barrier? Did you try one of our suggestions or do something different?

_____

_____

_____

_____

_____

_____

_____

2. WHAT IF WE ARE GROUPED TOGETHER BUT WORK INDEPENDENTLY ON TEACHING AND LEARNING?

Although the whole school is now invested in the PLC+ framework, you and your colleagues may find yourselves grouped together but working independently on your instruction. Quite literally, some of the teams simply gather together around a table while members work on "their own thing." In some cases, the PLC+'s data may indicate gains in student learning. This makes it especially hard for the instructional leadership team to spark a change. In other cases, there are missed opportunities for increasing gains in student learning.

Capitalize on Successes: The instructional leadership team must look for successful collaborations that have enhanced and enriched student learning. These successes are then celebrated and shared across the school during faculty meetings, at professional development days, and through the daily announcements. The specific collaboration is highlighted in each celebration.

Discuss the What and Why of Interdependence: Celebrating the successes of a PLC+ is not enough. The *activators* of each PLC+ should spend additional time engaging members in a dialogue about the value of interdependence. Using the hook of time, this conversation has become a professional learning opportunity for the PLC+.

Model: The instructional leadership team should not miss an opportunity to model the interdependence expected during the PLC+ process. In some cases, the team might use video as a means of professional development, as well as asking members to visit and observe the iterative work of teaching teams across the building.

Is this your PLC+? If so, how will you go around, go over, or remove the barrier? Did you try one of our suggestions or do something different?

_____

_____

_____

_____

_____

3. WHAT IF NO ONE STEPS UP TO ACTIVATE THE WORK OF THE PLC+?

Meet Ms. Johnston. Gina Johnston, when speaking of her Grade 4 PLC+, once said, "They almost instantly say 'not it' when we select the *activator* for the next PLC+ collaborative team meeting. I get so frustrated." Before her PLC+ was up and running, each member of her team expected someone else to take the lead. "Even I felt that, some days, I just expected someone else to do it." In some instances, and after much wait time, someone would begrudgingly volunteer. However, feeling compelled to volunteer to stop the awkward silence subsequently impeded the work of the PLC+. "If the teaching and learning of our students is paramount, I would think we would jump at the opportunity to activate the PLC+ work. That is simply not the case." After working with her mentor, Ms. Johnston and the team decided to map out a plan for making the activation fit more into the natural flow of the team's work. "We made it our own, if you will."

> **Solicit a Friend:** Rewind just a bit. Before Ms. Johnston could engage the team in the next two strategies for overcoming this barrier, she leveraged her credibility with two of her colleagues and asked them to step up for the next meeting. She solicited the help of a friend and colleague.

> **Define Expectations:** Ms. Johnston and her team devoted time to their own professional learning about both the roles within a PLC+ and the expectations associated with those roles. We addressed this topic early in this guide. As a group, members of Ms. Johnston's PLC+ agreed to a set of expectations that stayed in place the entire year so that as individuals stepped up to lead, the expectations were well defined and known in advance. If any adjustments were made, the whole team had to agree.

> **Reduce Outside Commitment:** As part of defining expectations, the team aimed to reduce the amount of outside work for the *activators*. This ensured that an *activator* could focus on his or her questioning and reflective practice and on the achievement of the goals of the particular PLC+ meeting.

Is this your PLC+? If so, how will you go around, go over, or remove the barrier? Did you try one of our suggestions or do something different?

_____

_____

_____

_____

_____

4. WHAT IF THE PLC+ IS INEFFECTIVE AT ACTIVATING DIALOGUE?

The algebra teachers at Mountain Springs High School are very strong—when it comes to content knowledge. The range of _pedagogical_ content knowledge across the department is more variable. However, that is not the problem. Each member of the algebra PLC+ team wants to enhance his or her learning outcomes. In mathematics, this includes both cognitive and affective outcomes. Yet when these teachers are together, they are unable to engage in effective dialogue, often sitting in silence. When they do engage in dialogue, the topics are superficial and lean toward complaining.

"All we end up doing is talking about what students don't know—multiplication facts, how to work with fractions—and how they simply want the answer. Then we shrug our shoulders until the end of our meeting." Simply put, the barrier for this PLC+ is that members are ineffective at activating the dialogue.

> **Gradual Release:** The instructional coach has decided to support this PLC+ given the individual strengths of the group. She decides to first model effectively activated dialogue using the PLC+ protocols through a gradual release approach: she activates the dialogue; they activate the dialogue with her; they activate the dialogue while she is in the PLC+ collaborative team meeting; and, finally, they activate the dialogue without her in the room.

> **Rotate Strategically:** In addition to receiving coaching, the PLC+ team decides to rotate responsibility for the activation of PLC+ collaborative meetings based on individual members' strengths. For example, if one member is strong at developing learning progressions, he or she would activate that particular conversation.

> **Build Capacity:** For the two previous strategies to help the team overcome this barrier, professional development on critical conversations and the PLC+ framework is necessary. This ongoing education not only provides important professional learning but builds the capacity of the PLC+ team.

Is this your PLC+? If so, how will you go around, go over, or remove the barrier? Did you try one of our suggestions or do something different?

_____

_____

_____

_____

5. WHAT IF THE PLC+ IS SO FOCUSED ON "GETTING IT DONE" THAT PROFESSIONAL LEARNING IS NOT VALUED?

The faculty at Atlantic Middle School focuses on the use of evidence-based practices. Over the years, the climate and culture changed, and teachers seek evidence for the strategies they use. What makes this middle school even more exceptional is its focus on having teachers read educational research and then work to incorporate the research into practice. Teams read articles on teaching and learning and then discuss how that would look in their classrooms. However, over time, the PLC+ team members have fallen into the trap of quickly reading the articles and then saying, "Let's plan this in tomorrow's lesson before I forget what I read." In other words, the attention is on getting through the article, plopping the idea into a lesson, and then moving on to the next task. This speed has created a barrier to the professional learning of the PLC+ collaborative teams and the individual teachers within the teams. The PLC+ team is focused on tasks—just get it done—but not focused on professional learning. Recognizing this barrier, one particular team has decided to get around it, or even knock it down, by implementing several strategies.

Shift the Focus to Students: One approach used by this PLC+ team is reframing the conversation to focus on the learners. Rather than focusing on what they will do in their lesson plans to implement the strategy, team members focus on discussing how the strategy will help learners.

Don't Focus on Teacher Dilemmas: Another approach team members used to get around this particular barrier was to move away from discussions about teacher dilemmas and toward explorations of how a particular strategy would help learners who are not making the expected progress in a specific content area.

Be Curious and Courageous: For members of this PLC+, being courageous and sharing their own curiosity about teaching and learning are important steps. Although this strategy seems a bit nebulous, for Atlantic Middle School it was successful—when an individual teacher simply expressed her curiosity about a specific challenge in her classroom and how an article supported her in addressing that challenge, others quickly followed along with their own contributions to the dialogue.

6. WHAT IF THE PLC+ MEMBERS BELIEVE THEY HAVE NO AUTHORITY TO MAKE "NEEDED" DECISIONS?

This is a tough one and one of our favorites to talk about in our own conversations regarding PLC+ work. When the PLC+ team at Desert View Elementary School decided it needed to slow down the unit based on initial assessment scores, the group worried that this was not a decision they had the authority to make. For example, one member said, "When the pacing guide says to move on, we do not have the option to slow down instruction. If someone does a walk-through and we are not on pace, we get dinged for it." This was the belief of most teachers in the building, and it paralyzed much of the work in the PLC+ framework. What works best for teaching and learning often requires decisions, tough ones at that. If the PLC+ collaborative teams, just like those at Desert View Elementary School, feel as if they cannot make those decisions, individual and collective efficacy will suffer. In some cases, teams have the authority to make those tough decisions (e.g., about the standardized testing schedule or school calendars and schedules). In many more cases, they have more authority than they realize—they simply have to exercise this authority in the right way. What do we do if there is no *perceived* authority within the PLC+ team to make decisions?

Seek the Go-Ahead: At Desert View Elementary School, as is the case at many other schools around the world, PLC+ members compiled a list of "things" they felt would work best for the teaching and learning of their students. From grouping to pacing, these "things" required certain overarching decisions. So one particular team met with their building-level leaders and shared this list, along with evidence documenting the need to make particular decisions. They sought the go-ahead, or green light, for these decisions.

Keep Brainstorming: As we might expect, not all of the decisions we seek the go-ahead for will get the green light. Thus, the PLC+ team is the ideal environment to keep brainstorming. If there are certain decisions that are beyond the authority of the group, devote time to brainstorming other options. Keeping the group focused on student learning during this brainstorm will prevent the dialogue from devolving into complaints.

Recognize, Re-Strategize, and Re-Empower: Along the same lines as brainstorming, activating dialogue around the authority to or to not make decisions should focus on recognizing the situation, rethinking strategies on how to address the situation given the current constraints, and focusing on what we *do* have the authority to do in our schools and classrooms.

REFLECTION

Is this your PLC+? If so, how will you go around, go over, or remove the barrier? Did you try one of our suggestions or do something different?

_____

_____

_____

_____

_____

7. WHAT IF THE PLC+ DOES NOT AGREE ON THE PROFESSIONAL LEARNING WITHIN THE PLC+ FRAMEWORK?

The transition from talking about instruction to agreeing on professional learning can produce barriers in the PLC+ framework. As teams talk about instruction, the conversation about professional learning arises, but not everyone may agree that professional learning is necessary. Just ask Bree Santiago and her Grade 1 PLC+. "Some of my colleagues felt their degrees and experience equipped them with all they needed to be successful," Bree said. "In fact, one team member said that parents and principals need to do their part." In another meeting, one of Bree's colleagues expressed her concern that "this educational jargon is not necessary. Plus, this is what we used to do in the eighties. Recycled ideas. Just wait and this will pass." Bree's PLC+ team members do not agree on the professional learning needed within the PLC+ framework.

Toss the Jargon, Pose the Questions: Ms. Santiago decided to toss the jargon associated with professional learning. She realized that word choice matters and thus consistently used words associated with student learning. In addition to the traditional approach of "telling," she also used questions focused on student learning to guide the group's professional learning.

Unpack the Meaning: Not all jargon can be avoided. In fact, concepts such as formative assessment, differentiation, clarity, and efficacy, to name a few, are not jargon. However, the meaning of those terms may not be clear to everyone. Although her approach met with resistance, Ms. Santiago decided to devote some of the professional learning to unpacking what was meant by each of the terms the group mislabeled as jargon.

Take the Paperwork Pledge: In addition to initiative fatigue, teachers can suffer from too much administrative work. So the thought of *more* paperwork can be daunting. Thus, Ms. Santiago made a personal commitment to members of her PLC+ collaborative team that the amount of PLC+ paperwork, including the paperwork associated with professional learning, would be either minimal or less than the amount they currently do. They would work smarter, not harder.

REFLECTION

Is this your PLC+? If so, how will you go around, go over, or remove the barrier? Did you try one of our suggestions or do something different?

_____

_____

_____

_____

8. WHAT IF THE PLC+ FOCUSES ON TEACHING AND LEARNING APPROACHES THAT WILL RESULT IN A MINIMAL IMPACT ON LEARNING?

As Harriet Tubman Elementary School and its PLC+ teams focused on writing strategies, several suggestions about how to move learning forward involved approaches or strategies that were not associated with a high impact on student learning. One of the members of the PLC+ put it this way, "The ideas we generated are things I have heard do not work in writing instruction. That is why we are not doing those things now." To be clear, this barrier to the work of the PLC+, and thus to student learning, most likely comes from not knowing. In other words, we could easily reframe this barrier and label it "not knowing what works best." On the other hand, teachers may be well aware of what works best, but they might not know how to match the right approach with the right content, student, and time. The following are some ways to overcome the barrier.

Start With Data: To ensure the teams at Harriet Tubman Elementary maximize their impact on student learning, all PLC+ collaborative team meetings are activated using data. Rather than selecting approaches or strategies, team members engage in dialogue about what the data say the particular tool must accomplish.

Determine Urgency: There are many different approaches and strategies that result in a high impact on student learning. When the dialogue shifts toward approaches that will result in minimal learning, guiding the conversation toward things that are the most urgently related to student progress will increase the odds of picking a high-yield approach.

Professional Development: This is the first time professional development has been explicitly identified as an approach to overcoming barriers. Members of this PLC+ collaborative team benefited from professional learning on evidence-based practices and what works best when.

REFLECTION

Is this your PLC+? If so, how will you go around, go over, or remove the barrier? Did you try one of our suggestions or do something different?

_____

_____

_____

_____

_____

_____

9.   WHAT IF THE PLC+ HAS MEMBERS THAT DO NOT WANT TO CHANGE?

Another favorite of ours! This is one of the toughest barriers to go around, go over, or remove. One of the social studies teachers at Toloache High School describes the barrier this way: "You can see them cross their arms right in the middle of a faculty meeting or team meeting. You know, right then and there, that they will be a tough sell—and even harder to move." Some of this resistance to change comes from teachers whose students have high test scores and do not want to rock the boat. However, as the instructional coach observes, "Another pocket of resistance comes from those who have done it this way for so long they are not interested in changing . . . even if it [what they have been doing] does not work." How do PLC+ teams activate dialogue that does not allow this particular barrier to stop permanently the work of the PLC+?

Scrap Consensus: The instructional leadership team responsible for implementing the PLC+ framework schoolwide decided early on to move forward without consensus. Moving forward the work of the PLC+ does not require 100 percent of the faculty and staff to be 100 percent on board. In the long term, yes, this is a realistic goal. However, consensus may come only after others experience or witness the success of the PLC+ approach (i.e., the move from individual to collective efficacy).

Connect Goals With Real Work: As we encounter those colleagues who are not willing to change, linking the everyday expected work of the classroom teacher to the goals of the PLC+ is paramount. This is not "one more thing" or "something totally different." This *is* the work. Describing the PLC+ framework as integral to the expectations of every school, classroom, and teacher will help overcome this barrier—it is something we should already be doing.

Think Big, Start Small: Big changes in the way we do business is a big turn-off to those already resistant to change. Keeping this in mind, the instructional team at Toloache High School decided to break down the work of the PLC+ framework into very small and doable chunks for those resistant to the change.

REFLECTION

Is this your PLC+? If so, how will you go around, go over, or remove the barrier? Did you try one of our suggestions or do something different?

_____

_____

_____

_____

_____

_____

10.   WHAT IF THE PLC+ IS SKEPTICAL OF ASSESSMENTS AND THEIR DATA?

As teachers review evidence, or data, about their teaching and learning, skepticism about an assessment can become a barrier to using these data either to encourage dialogue about how to move learning forward or as a means of determining who did and did not benefit from our teaching. Ms. Howser commented, "Some teachers simply don't have any faith in the assessments, or act like they don't. I hear comments about how we are better than any assessment can measure, or how the tests are just for the state." Whether these comments and the skepticism embedded in them constitute a genuine concern or a defense mechanism, not using the evidence and data available to us can bring most conversations about teaching and learning to a screeching halt. Ms. Howser decides to use several approaches that actually work to leverage the skepticism into productive dialogue.

Assessments *of*, *for*, and *as* Learning: Ms. Howser decided to use PLC+ conversations to compare and contrast the different relationships between assessments and learning. Awareness that an assessment can be used *as* and *for* the learning helped ease the defensiveness of her colleagues, as they previously had viewed assessments only as assessments *of* learning, and thus, of their instruction.

Professional Development: Ms. Howser noticed that her colleagues' understanding of "assessment *of, for,* and *as* learning" was full of misconceptions. Therefore, the PLC+ engaged in professional learning about formative and summative assessments, how to interpret assessment data, and how to use those data to make decisions.

Time Management: As a result of members' own professional learning, the PLC+ collaborative team began to look at ways to assess student learning without reducing instructional time. The team investigated the amount of time devoted to assessments— a major concern of the skeptics—and how to reduce that time by making assessment part of instruction.

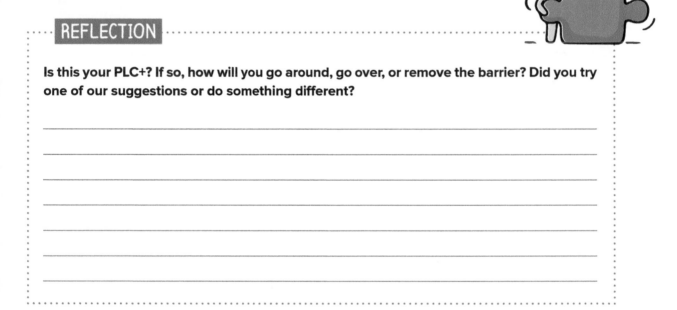

REFLECTION

Is this your PLC+? If so, how will you go around, go over, or remove the barrier? Did you try one of our suggestions or do something different?

_____

_____

_____

_____

_____

_____

_____

11. WHAT IF THE PLC+ ENGAGES IN DIALOGUE THAT IS SUPERFICIAL OR FOCUSES ON BLAME AND EXCUSES?

As we have highlighted in this particular part of the PLC+ framework, the question about who did and who did not benefit from instruction can lead to difficult conversations. There is a barrier that makes these conversations both difficult and unproductive: superficial conversations that spiral into blame and excuses. Before Ms. Lancaster and her team could discuss efficiently and effectively the growth and achievement of her learners, she had to stimulate dialogue with her colleagues to overcome this barrier. "There were times when we would avoid the obvious issue with our English language learners. We would stay on the surface, missing what was really going on. And when I tried to go deeper into the evidence, we would spiral into blaming parents, administrators, the central office . . . One day we blamed our politicians. That was a tough day." After seeking the advice of her mentor and colleague at another school, Ms. Lancaster used a series of strategies to get the dialogue back on track.

Paraphrase and Question: During difficult conversations when blame and excuses permeated the PLC+ collaborative team meeting, Ms. Lancaster would paraphrase the comments or side comments of her colleagues and then ask a probing question. Most of the questions focused on helping her colleagues differentiate between what they could and could not control.

Validate and Verify: When the dialogue in her PLC+ resulted in one member of the team making an assertion about individual students and their circumstances, Ms. Lancaster would respond with a request that the comment be verified with the evidence. With time, others engaged in the same practice to ensure the dialogue was evidence driven and not dictated by generalities and blame.

Clear Focus on the Outcome: At the start of each PLC+ collaborative team meeting, Ms. Lancaster would provide a clear outcome for the meeting that was specific to a determination of who did and did not benefit from learning. When the dialogue seemed to move off track, she would play out a "what if" scenario that focused on the team members changing their instructional approach so as to benefit more students, "What if we . . . ?"

············ REFLECTION ···

Is this your PLC+? If so, how will you go around, go over, or remove the barrier? Did you try one of our suggestions or do something different?

_____

_____

_____

_____

_____

_____

12. WHAT IF THE PLC+ MEETING IS MANDATED AND NOT VOLUNTARY?

Yeah, this is a good one too. Engaging in a task that is mandated and not something we willfully want to engage in has a significant influence on our efforts and attitudes toward that task. At Williams Elementary School, the mandate from the two administrators to "activate" a PLC+ elicited similar responses. Ms. Wright, one of the two *activators*, did what she was mandated to do, but no more. She said, "When we were made to participate in the PLC+ framework, we simply did what we were supposed to do, answered the five questions, and got it over with." This barrier will move the PLC+ framework from an iterative process that reflects how schools and classrooms should do business to simply one more initiative that has to get done. In some cases, this feeling of compulsory participation can lead to undermining respect and to "behind-the-scenes" campaigning against a process that should maximize our impact through teaching and learning. Ms. Wright and the other *activator* of the PLC+ framework had to make some adjustments to the activation of each part of the process.

Distinguish the Act of Resistance From the Person: One of the first steps in responding to this barrier is an internal strategy for the PLC+ *activator*— separate the behavior of resistance from the person doing the resisting. Don't make it personal or take it personally. There is something about the work that is threatening to our colleagues, but their resistance does not make them "bad people."

Acknowledge and Diffuse: Seeing the resistance as separate from the person will allow *activators* to acknowledge the resistance professionally and to begin to dialogue about how to move forward embracing the resistance. Having someone on the team who constantly asks *why* can be healthy; that person can help the PLC+ avoid the other barriers presented in this book. We all have colleagues whose role is to say, "Yeah, but," to any idea. We are, more often than not, very grateful they are on the team.

Discover a Solution, Don't Defend One: For every "Yeah, but," we should embrace both the resistance and the fact that this opposition is a mandate, i.e., a clear instruction toward finding a solution. Use the exception to inspire a dialogue to find solutions, brainstorming ways to move teaching and learning forward within the framework of the mandate. Again, this is not a bad thing unless we let the dissatisfaction of the mandate hijack the dialogue away from teaching and learning.

REFLECTION

Is this your PLC+? If so, how will you go around, go over, or remove the barrier? Did you try one of our suggestions or do something different?

_____

_____

_____

_____

_____

_____

_____

13.   WHAT IF THE PLC+ HAS A MISALIGNMENT BETWEEN INTENTIONS AND ACTIONS?

Intentions and actions are not always aligned. As Mr. Flynn and his PLC+ members depart each meeting, they have a clear and actionable plan for moving their work from dialoguing about teaching and learning to putting that dialogue into action. This has not always been the case. "When we first began this work, we would leave the collaborative team meetings with a rubric, an authentic task, and ways to meet the needs of our learners. When we talked again, some colleagues had not done anything." Mr. Flynn shared that his colleagues would either drop the ball or were too busy to start this or that initiative, but planned on starting next week. This barrier, whether erected intentionally or unintentionally, involves PLC+ members expressing good intentions within the framework but taking no action to back up those intentions. Thus, Mr. Flynn and others activating the collaborative team meetings had to take a different approach.

> **Create an Actionable Plan:** Rather than talking about the actionable items and assuming everyone on the PLC+ team was good to go, Mr. Flynn ended each collaborative team meeting with a clear actionable plan that had dates and specific deliverables. Although these action plans were eventually done away with (through scaffolding learning), the explicit nature of the plan helped align intentions with actions.

> **Codesign a Lesson:** To further support colleagues who struggled with moving from intention to action, the *activators* of each PLC+ collaborative team meeting would expedite the codesign of a lesson, assessment, approach, or strategy within the team, so each member could leave with that artifact ready to use.

> **Model and Debrief:** As part of the learning walks and video analysis of teaching implemented in the district, Mr. Flynn and his PLC+ team decided to model the actionable items developed in their time together. They would model the ideas, and, either through learning walks or video analysis, they would debrief with their PLC+ colleagues. This provided colleagues with concrete examples of what the actionable items might look like in the classroom.

REFLECTION

Is this your PLC+? If so, how will you go around, go over, or remove the barrier? Did you try one of our suggestions or do something different?

_____

_____

_____

_____

_____

14. WHAT IF PLC+ MEMBERS WORK IN ISOLATION AND HAVE TROUBLE ESTABLISHING INTERDEPENDENCE?

When a team is made up of singletons, meaning teachers who do not share in the teaching of a common course or program, it can be a challenge to activate the learning of the group. It is essential to find common challenges that unite the team, challenges that don't shoehorn team members but that actually empower them to see where their interdependence lies.

Search for Commonalities Versus Differences: One strategy *activators* can employ during meetings is to have certain members of the team **present** their challenges while other members serve as **consultants**. This is similar to what happens in other professions, such as when a doctor presents the case of a patient and that doctor's professional opinion and diagnosis to other physicians, seeking their collective expertise to determine the best course of action.

- This approach can be especially effective for vertical teams whose members teach the same subject but who don't share in teaching the same specific course; team members make excellent consultants because they all have a background in the subject matter being taught (e.g., biology, chemistry, physics, or algebra), so they can support their peers in finding solutions.

- *Activators* can drive deeper ownership into these discussions by making sure team members are aware of their interdependence. How well students do in freshman algebra or biology, for example, will directly impact how they perform in algebra or chemistry in their sophomore and junior years.

- Instead of dwelling on the obvious differences the team has, examine how your PLC+ team can develop a consistent practice of establishing time—or even entire meetings—so that members can present their challenges. The role of other team members is to offer support, expertise, and strategies. The *activator's* role is to remind the team that while there are differences in the actual courses members teach, there is commonality in the expertise they share.

REFLECTION

Is this your PLC+? If so, how will you go around, go over, or remove the barrier? Did you try one of our suggestions or do something different?

_____

_____

_____

Be the Catalyst: Instead of using the relational challenges or barriers discussed in this chapter as a diagnostic manual, one approach is to use them, and other scenarios that you come up with, as professional learning opportunities. Make copies of the previously described situations, *but not the recommended solutions*, and cut them up so that each situation is on its own strip of paper. Place these into baggies so that each member of your PLC+ or every faculty member in your school has a baggie of scenarios. You can put different scenarios in each bag so that individuals or PLC+ teams have different scenarios to reflect on. Have individuals pull strips from their baggies and discuss strategies for addressing the situations—first in a small group and then with all who are present.

Record these ideas on poster paper or in an online document so that they can be shared with all faculty members in every PLC+. This process might help your colleagues see themselves in some or all of the scenarios without feeling called out. You might even recognize yourself in a few! This supports reflective practice.

NOTES

_____
_____
_____
_____
_____
_____
_____
_____
_____
_____
_____
_____
_____
_____
_____
_____
_____
_____
_____

Be the Catalyst: We are now asking you for a favor. As you transition into the next and final part of this book, we invite you to share any adaptations, ideas, or reflections that you think are missing from this work. Using our emails, which can be found in this guide as well as in the other PLC+ books, share with us! What do you think we have missed? The only way to have a true impact on teaching and learning is through our collective efficacy.

_____

_____

_____

_____

_____

_____

_____

_____

_____

_____

_____

_____

_____

_____

_____

_____

_____

_____

_____

_____

_____

_____

_____

_____

_____

_____

_____

Part 8

ACTIVATNG CONVERSATIONS FOCUSED ON EQUITY

One of the hardest tasks for any PLC+ *activator* is supporting conversations related to equity. Honest dialogue about how aspects of race and ethnicity, socioeconomic status, gender, sexual identity and orientation, and other demographic characteristics may be impacting achievement in our classrooms is often uncomfortable for educators. This kind of dialogue deserves a separate part in this guide. This challenge is compounded by the fact that, in many cases, honest conversations about equity have never happened before, and people feel ill equipped to participate in them, much less activate them. However, conversations about equity are the ones we *must* have in education. The potential for these conversations to have an impact on student learning and on the overall lives of our learners is tremendous, especially at the PLC+ table. As you and your colleagues determine what actions and strategies best support all of your learners, having intentional conversations around equity provides the mechanism that doesn't just guarantee all students will succeed but rather "that the students of greatest need receive the greatest level of support" (Singleton, 2014, p. 45). Glenn Singleton provides a protocol with four guiding considerations that will help focus and support teams and *activators* in conversations about equity:

- Stay engaged

- Experience discomfort

- Speak your truth

- Expect and accept non-closure

See *The PLC+ Playbook* (page 11).

Be the Catalyst: Take a moment and flag all the tools in *The PLC+ Playbook* that support our work to achieve equity for our learners. We engaged in a similar "Be the Catalyst" task in Part 1 of this guide (see page 16). Use that as a resource. Also, locate the pages in the core book that unpack equity across the five guiding questions. Combining these resources and the expertise in your PLC+, design an engaging task that you and your PLC+ can use to activate and build background knowledge on equity. What does equity mean? What does the term imply? How do we take the term equity and put it into action? Use the space provided to plan out this task.

_____

_____

_____

_____

_____

_____

_____

_____

_____

_____

_____

_____

_____

_____

_____

_____

_____

_____

_____

_____

_____

_____

Using Singleton's four guiding considerations, let's walk through a series of vignettes that provide examples and guidance for all of us on how to frame dialogue in our PLC+. Note how the *activator* in each instance frames the discussion or addresses comments from team members and how that drastically impacts where the discussion is headed.

VIGNETTE 1: STAYING ENGAGED

The first step in activating the protocol is making sure team members stay engaged. When conversations are difficult and results challenge us, it is easy to *check out*. At times, this is done overtly; individuals will demonstrate through body language or even verbally their discomfort and their desire to deflect blame to external factors. Other times, members will simply stay quiet, wait for someone else to address the issue, and hope that the meeting or at least this part of the meeting will simply run out of time. Examine the following vignette:

Samantha (Activator):	As I mentioned in the email regarding today's meeting, we are going to look at the results from our recent assessment specifically through an equity lens. As you can see, we have a significant gap with our African American students, as well as with students that are below the poverty level. We need to have honest dialogue today about what we see in the results, why we feel we are seeing the results we are, and what action steps we need to take moving forward. I have created a list of students for each of us. . . . [She is stopped before she can finish by Bill.]
Bill:	I get what you are trying to say and get us to look at, but I can tell you that I would like to know what some of these students' parents are doing when they go home or how involved they are in their kids' education. I mean, as I look at this list, I can't remember any of these parents at open house.
Steve:	I agree. I mean I can only do so much as a teacher. It's really challenging when we are required to teach some pretty complex concepts and too many of our students don't have access to support at home. I struggle knowing what to do to ensure my kids are learning what they need to.

Here is where the *activator's* role is critical. First and foremost, establishing norms related to conversations around equity is an important first step. See "Setting Norms for Our Ways of Work" in *The PLC+ Playbook* (pages 35–37).

Second, we must challenge notions that equity gaps are beyond the scope of the team's influence or responsibility. *Activators* must do so in a way that respects people's dignity, so they don't feel threatened or attacked, while still ensuring that the conversation stays focused on awareness, actions, and solutions—instead of on excuses or the external factors that might be to blame.
Here is an example of Samantha doing just that:

Samantha (Activator):	Bill and Steve, I hear you both . . . I do. But I can't say I agree that a lack of parental involvement is the reason we are seeing this gap. We know we have students who

See *The PLC+ Playbook* (pages 35–37).

(Continued)

(Continued)

are doing well, and their parents are nonfactors. We also have students who are struggling, and they have access to support both in and out of the school. Let's make sure to adhere to our process norm here—in equity conversations, we do not deflect by presenting reasons that are beyond our scope of influence or control to explain any learning gaps we are seeing. We have to be careful that we don't generalize or make assumptions about our students or their families. Let's take a look at the data again with a fresh lens and capitalize on the brainpower of this team as we explore what skills students are lacking and what might be impeding their proficiency. Then we can brainstorm possible strategies to close the gap. Fair enough?

VIGNETTE 2: EXPERIENCING DISCOMFORT

Conversations around equity are not easy, nor should they be. A student's educational trajectory has great influence on her or his life trajectory. Supporting all students on the path to growth is a responsibility all teachers must embrace, and to do so, teachers need to be prepared to have honest discussions with their peers—to make sure student learning and progressive development happen. But discomfort can get in the way.

Let's first look at a situation in which an *activator's* fear of discomfort undermines a discussion about equity:

Manuel (Activator): We need to examine the results of our recent post-assessments, and we need to do so with an equity lens. We need to be honest with each other in how we look at these results in terms of our different subgroups of students. I have taken the time to break down our results by ethnicity, SES [socioeconomic status], gender, IEP, and ELL. Our African American students and students in the free or reduced-cost lunch program did not do nearly as well as the rest of the students. Our students as a whole did very well when we look at overall scores, so let's make sure we stay focused there and don't feel bad about where we are falling short with some of our students.

In this example, Manuel is *not* guiding the team to have a real discussion related to the equity gap presented in the data. Because he is not ready to experience discomfort, Manuel undermines the critical goal of the PLC+: examining the growth and achievement of *all* students. PLC+ teams cannot live in a "land of nice" and expect to have the impact on *all* student learning that they hope and aspire to achieve. Part of the *activator's* job is to use the PLC+'s strategies and protocols so that conversations are structured and have a safe platform to exist. Dismissal of looking at data for any student or group of students is an unacceptable practice.

Now, listen to Manuel work through his fear and discomfort to activate his PLC+ successfully by encouraging an honest discussion of teaching and learning for *all* students:

Manuel (Activator):	We need to examine the results of our recent post-assessments, and we need to do so with an equity lens. We need to be honest with each other in how we look at these results in terms of our different subgroups of students. I have taken the time to break down our results by ethnicity, SES [socioeconomic status], gender, IEP, and ELL. As you can see by these data, while we can celebrate the improvements we've made in terms of our overall impact on student achievement, we have some serious gaps when we break results down by subgroup. Our African American students and students in the free or reduced-cost lunch program did not do nearly as well as the rest of the students. We have to acknowledge that problem and then approach how we look for solutions that will support all of our students. If we want results we haven't had yet, we will need to do things we haven't done yet. I've taken the time to look into a few resources that might help us adapt the instructional approaches we are currently using to better serve these two groups of students. Does anyone know of other resources or perspectives that might help?

Notice the difference in Manuel's approach. He doesn't undermine the overall success they have had with the majority of students, but he moves the conversation beyond that success to a deeper conversation about the students who did not learn. Manuel is honest and direct in acknowledging that the results are going to cause some discomfort, but his approach will allow the team truly to begin a conversation on equity in a manner that will promote dialogue and discussions leading to action. And he is fully prepared with tools to help activate his team in this direction.

VIGNETTE 3: SPEAKING THE TRUTH

Activating team members to speak their truth involves making sure people feel safe being honest. Silence or lack of dialogue should not be perceived as agreement.

In the following scenarios, note how the two conversations are framed differently by the *activator*, and also note the different results that follow:

Anna (Activator):	We need to examine the results of our recent post-assessments, and we need to do so with an equity lens. We need to be honest with each other in how we look at these results in terms of our different subgroups of students. I have taken the time to break down our results by ethnicity, SES [socioeconomic status], gender, IEP, and ELL. Our African American students and students in the free or reduced-cost lunch program did not do nearly as well as the rest of the students. Our students as a whole did very well when we look at overall scores, so let's make sure we stay focused there and don't feel bad about where we are falling short with some of our students. Is there anything you see that specifically catches your attention . . . or something anyone would like to share to get the conversation going? [After a period of silence] Harold . . . Anything?

(Continued)

(Continued)

Harold: Well, I am not sure how to think about these subgroup results yet. I mean
                           of course we would all agree we aren't happy or satisfied with them, but we
                           are all working hard and doing our best. Maybe we need to make sure we
                           have the kids practice more before the next summative. [Again, a period of
                           silence follows.]

Anna (Activator):   Thanks Harold, are there any other thoughts to contribute to what Harold sug-
                           gested? [No additional comments are offered.] . . . Okay, then I am going to
                           guess we are all good with giving our kids extra practice before the summative.
                           Does anyone have practice tests already made that we can use?

See *The PLC+*
Playbook (Module 22,
pages 149–150).

The *activator* must set the stage for both the actual conversation related to the data
or evidence being examining as well as for the affective, emotional side of this discussion about the results. Here again is an example showing that having process
norms to use prior to and during the conversation can be extremely helpful in ensuring honest dialogue. This is also a time to frame the discussion in terms of our honest
and perceived reality. In what ways are we prepared to support those of our students
who show the greatest need? (See Module 22 of *The PLC+ Playbook*.)

Now let's look at how this conversation might go differently:

Anna (Activator):   We need to examine the results of our recent post-assessments, and we need to
                           do so with an equity lens. We need to be honest with each other in how we look
                           at these results in terms of our different groups of students. I have taken the time
                           to break down our results by ethnicity, SES [socioeconomic status], gender, IEP,
                           and ELL. Our African American students and students in the free or reduced-cost
                           lunch program did not do nearly as well as the rest of the students. We have to
                           acknowledge that problem and then approach how we look for solutions that
                           will support all of our students. If we want results we haven't had yet, we will
                           need to do things we haven't done yet. While we are all working very hard, we
                           aren't moving some students the way we need to. I know it isn't easy to look at
                           data and know that we're not making the impact we want to, but if we approach
                           the conversation with honesty and use the expertise of the whole team, I think
                           we will find new strategies and ideas to consider as we move forward with our
                           instruction. I think some of the questions in Module 22 can help shape our dis-
                           cussion. I want to remind us that, in our PLC+, we recognize and value all ideas
                           and contributions. We also acknowledge that sometimes vulnerability is neces-
                           sary in order for us to grow. I'll pose some questions to get us started:

                           •   Given these gaps we are seeing, how confident are we feeling as a team
                               in our instructional abilities?

                           •   How confident are we feeling in removing some of the barriers to student
                               learning we know are present for our students of color or our students
                               living in poverty?

	• How confident are we feeling in our ability as a team to design and deliver effective interventions for these students, interventions specifically related to the gaps we are seeing? [After a period of silence] Bill . . . do you mind getting us started with your initial thoughts?
Bill:	Sure. And Anna, thanks for setting up the conversation the way you did and acknowledging we are all working very hard. It helps, I think, to not pretend that isn't the case or that we haven't tried supporting all of our students. For whatever reason, what we are doing or have done so far isn't working or hasn't worked yet. I do feel confident to address some of the gaps we are seeing and am prepared with ideas and strategies to share, but for some of the others, I do feel a little out of strategies and could really use some ideas and support from everyone here. [There is a positive and collective murmur of agreement from the group.]
Anna (Activator):	Thanks Bill very much for sharing that and getting that out in the open. I too feel that way. I mean I have a lot of strategies I use often for all of our students when they aren't progressing, but my bag isn't unlimited, and I feel very vulnerable as I look at these results . . . in terms of not knowing how to move forward. [There is collective agreement indicated by nods, positive affirmations, and body language across the team.] I have to tell you . . . I am very proud of us for how we are approaching this topic and conversation. I don't think this would have been the case last semester. We really have grown together and are prepared to take on any challenge we come across. Let's dig in!

VIGNETTE 4: EXPECTING AND ACCEPTING NON-CLOSURE

Finally, *activators* must guide their teams to expect and accept non-closure. Singleton (2014, p. 55) notes that achieving true equity for all students must be a moral imperative. There are no quick fixes, and solutions aren't found easily; instead, they are found in the dialogue itself.

Char (Activator):	Okay. So, we all agree we need to dig in to looking at the growth and achievement of subgroups of students. We'll explore trends and talk about strategies that have had a positive impact on student learning. We'll also focus on how we are going to address some of the gaps we see in the data.
Dave:	Well, it's clear the analysis of text is a very low data point for our ELL students. I see stamina as a big factor. I mean, they will never reach proficiency or mastery if they give up, or if we provide only short windows of time for reading in class. I propose a big shift in action . . . we allow for more time, say at least 35 minutes, for those students to read two to three times per week. Then we can help them get through the longer passages of text so they will be better able to analyze what they are reading. [There is collective agreement, and the body language of several members conveys finality in the discussion.]

(Continued)

(Continued)

Char (Activator):	Okay, Dave, and thank you for sharing that insight as well as that possible strategy as a starting point. But I think we have to dig deeper and talk about how we will support students as they are reading. It can't just be more time. Lydia, what are your thoughts?
Lydia:	Well, I do agree with Dave, about both analysis of text being low and reading stamina being an issue, and I think some of our students need more sustained reading time built into lesson planning. I do think we need to be more intentional in supporting all students in having some choice in what they read. If stamina is what we are striving for, then cramming books they have no interest in or desire to work through is going to be a dead end.
Dave:	I agree.
Char (Activator):	Also, we have to do more than just provide more time. What are the actual skill deficits that we can focus on and support learning to address? Dawn . . . do you have any ideas?
Dawn:	I do love the ideas we are sharing and agree with both Dave and Lydia. One, we need to get the students' interest peaked in what they read, but also provide some real intentional support for helping them analyze texts. I think we need to provide some very intentional anchor charts with guiding questions that we can develop as a team. I am talking about some questions that literally help them by almost giving them the inferences to look for in the text . . . specific page numbers for those who lack that skill. We need to help them get it right initially and develop some confidence and then scaffold this learning as they develop more skills. Again, this is where we can differentiate based on the impact the support has on supporting the growth of our students' ability to analyze texts. The goal is to remove the supports eventually, once the academic readiness is established. We don't want to offer supports that are no longer needed and unintentionally disempower a student through spoon-feeding. This is going to be messy, and we can't assume it's simply going to lead all kids to the promised land overnight.
Char (Activator):	Dawn, so well put. This is a journey. Let's determine what exactly we are committing to, how we will divide labor in developing some of these tools we are talking about, and what we will look for in student work and student voice evidence to know this is working.
Dave:	[Smiling] You know, I feel we are becoming very authentically collectively efficacious! [The team laughs in acknowledgment.]

Here is your final task in this guide. Using the highlighter, marker, or tabs that have been with you from the beginning of this journey, make notes on the above vignettes. Do you see yourself in those vignettes? Highlight it! Do you see your colleagues? Mark it. Do you see areas of opportunity? Tab it!

TABLE 8.1

USE THE QUESTIONS IN THE CHART BELOW TO CONSIDER HOW YOUR PLC+ WILL ADDRESS THE ISSUE OF EQUITY IN TEACHING AND LEARNING.	
EQUITY AND YOUR PLC+	
How does your team currently address conversations related to equity?	
How could the above four protocol considerations guide your conversations related to equity?	

CLOSING REMARKS

Whew, that was a journey. The good news is you have grown professionally as an *activator*. **And, if we have developed this guide well, you have built capacity in your colleagues so that you will spend a significant amount of time in a room full of *activators*.** That is the power of PLC+. When we, as professionals, leverage the individual efficacy in the room into a collective efficacy, driven by high expectations and the unquenchable thirst for equity, we have the power to impact the teaching and learning in our schools and classrooms, not by chance, but by design. Oh, if you think this journey is done, you are mistaken. However, you and your colleagues have the tools to meet the needs of all learners now, next year, and for many years to come. The learners may change, come with different opportunities and needs, but the power in your PLC+ is the same. Ensuring that learners are better off at the end of the day just because they spent time with you and your colleagues is the ultimate goal. The answer for attaining that goal is in the room. Look around you: the answer to high-impact teaching and learning is already in the room—and not in the pages of this, or *any*, book. That answer is the plus in PLC+. **The plus is you.**

REFERENCES

Bloom, S.L., & Farragher, B. (2013). *Restoring sanctuary: A new operating system for trauma-informed systems of care*. New York: Oxford University Press.

Brown, A.L., & Campione, J. (1996). Psychological theory and the design of innovative-learning environments: On procedures, principles and systems. In L. Schauble & R. Glaser (Eds.), *Innovations in learning: New environments for education* (pp. 289–325). Hillsdale, NJ: Erlbaum.

Brown, M.W., & Edelson, D.C. (2001, April) Teaching by design: Curriculum design as a lens on instructional practice. Paper presented at the Annual Meeting of the American Educational Research Association, Seattle, WA.

Cordray, D.S., & Pion, G.M. (2006). Treatment strength and integrity: Models and methods. In R.R. Bootzin & P.E. McKnight (Eds.), *Strengthening research methodology: Psychological measurement and evaluation* (pp. 103–124). Washington, DC: American Psychological Association.

Engel, M., Claessens, A., & Finch, M.A. (2013). Teaching students what they already know? The (mis)alignment between mathematics instructional content and student knowledge in kindergarten. *Educational Evaluation and Policy Analysis, 35*(2), 157–178.

Fisher, D., Frey, N., Almarode, J., Flories, K., & Nagel, D. (2020a). *PLC+: Better decisions and greater impact by design*. Thousand Oaks, CA: Corwin.

Fisher, D., Frey, N., Almarode, J., Flories, K., & Nagel, D. (2020b). *The PLC+ playbook, Grades K–12: A hands-on guide to collectively improving student learning*. Thousand Oaks, CA: Corwin.

Garmston, R.J. (2012). *Unlocking group potential to improve schools*. Thousand Oaks, CA: SAGE.

Garmston, R.J., & Wellman, B.M. (2009). *The adaptive school: A sourcebook for developing collaborative groups* (2nd ed.). Lanham, MD: Rowman & Littlefield.

Garmston, R.J., & Wellman, B.M. (2016). *The adaptive school: A sourcebook for developing collaborative groups* (3rd ed.). Lanham, MD: Rowman & Littlefield.

Harris, A., & Jones, M. (2010). Professional learning communities and system improvement. *Improving Schools, 13*(2), 172–181.

Kayser, T. (1990). *Mining group gold: How to cash in on the collaborative power of a group*. El Segundo, CA: Serif Publishing.

Levi, D. (2014). *Group dynamics for teams* (4th ed.). Thousand Oaks, CA: SAGE.

Logan, D., King, J.P., & Fischer-Wright, H. (2011). *Tribal leadership: Leveraging natural groups to build a thriving organization*. New York, NY: Harper Business.

MacDonald, E. (2013). *The skillful team leader: A resource for overcoming hurdles to professional learning for student achievement*. Thousand Oaks, CA: Corwin.

Marzano, R.J. (2003). *What works in schools: Translating research into action.* Alexandria, VA: ASCD.

McDonald, S.-K. (2009). Scale-up as a framework for intervention, program, and policy evaluation research. In G. Sykes, B. Schneider, & D.N. Plank (Eds.), *Handbook of education policy research* (pp. 191–208). Washington, DC: American Educational Research Association.

Penuel, W.R., Frank, K.A., Fishman, B.J., Sabelli, N., & Cheng, B. (2009). *Expanding the scope of implementation research in education to inform design.* Menlo Park, CA: SRI International.

Penuel, W.R., Phillips, R.S., & Harris, C.J. (2014). Analysing teachers' curriculum implementation from integrity and actor-oriented perspectives. *Journal of Curriculum Studies, 46,* 751–777.

Sinek, S. (2009). *Start with why. How great leaders inspire everyone to take action.* New York, NY: Penguin.

Singleton, G. (2014). *Courageous conversations about race: A field guide for achieving equity in schools.* Thousand Oaks, CA: Corwin.

Spotsylvania County Public Schools. (2016). *Framework for teaching and learning.* Retrieved from https://www.spotsylvania.k12.va.us/cms/lib/VA01918722/Centricity/Domain/281/TL Framework 2016.pdf.

INDEX

CORWIN
A SAGE Publishing Company

Helping educators make the greatest impact

CORWIN HAS ONE MISSION: to enhance education through intentional professional learning.

We build long-term relationships with our authors, educators, clients, and associations who partner with us to develop and continuously improve the best evidence-based practices that establish and support lifelong learning.

3 Ways to get started with PLC+

The **PLC+ framework** is designed to refresh current collaborative structures and support teachers' decision making in the context of individual and collective efficacy, expectations, equity, and the activation of their own learning.

1

Watch the PLC+ Webinar

Preview the PLC+ framework with thought leaders Douglas Fisher and Nancy Frey.

To view the webinar, visit corwin.com/PLCWebinar

2

Attend an Event

Attendees will walk away with a better understanding of the PLC+ framework's potential impact, steps for implementation, and how to build individual and collective efficacy as well as teacher credibility.

For more information, visit corwin.com/PLCInstitutes

3

Meet With a Senior Professional Learning Advisor

Our Senior Professional Learning Advisors will help assess your current PLC structures or discuss options for implementation if your school is new to PLCs. Our customizable PLC+ PD Series ensures better decisions and greater impact by design.

For more information, visit corwin.com/PLCPD

Visit **corwin.com/PLC+** to learn more

CORWIN PLC+